D0665724

FORWARD TOGETHER

A New Vision for Senior Adult Ministry

Compiled by
John G. "Jay" Johnston

LifeWay Press
Nashville, Tennessee

ISBN: 0-7673-3115-X
Dewey Decimal Classification: 259.3
Subject Heading: CHURCH WORK WITH THE ELDERLY

This book is the text for three Leadership and Skill Development diploma plans
of the Christian Growth Study Plan. The courses are LS-0034 for Senior Adult Ministry,
LS-0067 for Family Ministry, and LS-0083 for Church Leadership.

Unless otherwise noted, Scripture quotations are from the Holy Bible,
New International Version, copyright © 1973, 1978, 1984
by International Bible Society.

Scripture quotations marked KJV are from the *King James Version.*

Printed in the United States of America

LifeWay Press
127 Ninth Avenue, North
Nashville, Tennessee 37234-0151

Contents

Meet the Writers

These contributors are on the staff of LifeWay Christian Resources of the Southern Baptist Convention, Nashville, Tennessee:

John G. "Jay" Johnston, *Chapter 1*
Training and Enrichment Manager, Discipleship and Family Adult Department, Discipleship and Family Development Division

Larry Mizell, *Chapter 2 and Chapter 9*
Senior Adult Enrichment Event Specialist, Discipleship and Family Adult Department, Discipleship and Family Development Division

David Apple, *Chapter 3 and Chapter 5*
Adult Lead Consultant, Leadership and Evangelism Department, Bible Teaching-Reaching Division

Ralph Hodge, *Chapter 4*
Discipleship Design Specialist, Discipleship and Family Leadership Department, Discipleship and Family Development Division

John Franklin, *Chapter 4*
Prayer/Discipleship Specialist, Discipleship and Family Adult Department, Discipleship and Family Development Division

Robert Sheffield, *Chapter 5*
Church Consultant, Deacon and Pastoral Ministries and Church Administration, Pastor-Staff Leadership Department, Church Leadership Services Division

John Garner, *Chapter 8*
Church Recreation Program Director, Pastor-Staff Leadership Department, Church Leadership Services Division

J. David Carter, *Chapter 10*
Lead Stewardship Specialist, Church Stewardship Services, Church Leadership Services Division

Joseph F. Northcut, *Chapter 11*
Discipleship and Family Specialist, Discipleship and Family Adult Department, Discipleship and Family Development Division

Betty Hassler, *Chapter 4, Leader Guide*
Design Editor, Discipleship and Family Adult Department, Discipleship and Family Development Division

Other contributors:

Bill Bacon, *Chapter 6*
Minister of Music, First Baptist Church, Clinton, Mississippi

Loren A. Williams, *Chapter 7*
Retired, Church Services and Community Ministries Department, Collin Baptist Association, McKinney, Texas

Editorial Team:

Betty Hassler, *Editor*
Linda Coombs, *Assistant Editor*
Leslie Irwin, *Manuscript Assistant*
Paula Savage, *Art Director*

Introduction

When I wrote *How to Minister to Senior Adults in the Church*, published in 1980, no one expected it to be the manual for senior adult ministry for almost 20 years! Now ministers, staff, and lay leaders have a new guidebook for improving and expanding church-based ministries with senior adults.

From 1976-1989 I was manager of the former senior adult section of the Family Ministry Department, Sunday School Board (now LifeWay Christian Resources) of the Southern Baptist Convention. During those years, the nation began to awaken to a realization that a growing percentage of the population was age 60 or older. Implications of this trend brought varied responses from government agencies and private organizations as they sought to determine what this demographic change meant to their constituencies. Southern Baptists have been in the forefront in this ministry and in assisting and encouraging churches and senior adults in this pursuit.

Church leaders are becoming more aware of opportunities to minister with, by, and to this growing age group. Many churches have responded with ministries designed to assist senior adults to enjoy the high quality of life to which Jesus referred: "I have come that they may have life, and have it to the full" (John 10:10).

In *Forward Together* writers from various perspectives provide practical suggestions which are adaptable to all churches. This holistic approach will result in a more comprehensive ministry to meet needs and interests of senior adults.

The reader is called to an awareness not only of the continuation of the phenomenon of an aging population but also of the changing nature of the senior adult population as a new generation moves into it. This is vital to keeping senior adult ministries viable and meaningful to all senior adults.

Horace L. Kerr

Chapter 1

A New Vision for Senior Adult Ministry

by John G. "Jay" Johnston

A Profile of Today's Seniors: 65 and Older
Impact of Baby Boomer Seniors
Implications for the Church
Mobilize Senior Adults for Ministry
Cast a New Vision

They are everywhere. You see them at grocery stores, sporting events, concerts, churches, parks, shopping malls, restaurants, and schools. They make up more than 12 percent of the U.S. population. As they continue to influence our country, society, and churches, senior adults will be a dynamic and influential force in the shaping of the 21st century.

Let's examine more closely the generations who are 65 and older and then look at the new crop of baby boomer seniors who began turning 50 in 1996. How are the seniors of today and tomorrow alike? different? What programs and ministries appeal to each group? How will the church need to change and adapt as the boomer seniors become more numerous?

Churches have a unique opportunity to engage and empower this resourceful army of present and potential volunteers. Seniors care greatly about the world they live in. They have a vast storehouse of knowledge and experience. To mobilize senior adults for ministry, we must understand who they are and how they are changing.

A Profile of Today's Seniors: 65 and Older

Stereotypes and myths about senior adults persist despite evidence to the contrary. The image of persons 65 and older as frail, hard of hearing, nearsighted, passive, and docile may characterize some seniors; but for the most part they are very active, alert, and eager to learn. They travel, volunteer, and lead independent lives with a measure of financial security unknown to previous generations. Instead of being cared for by family members, many in this age group are caregivers for adult children and grandchildren.

Today's senior adults have a strong work ethic that has served them well through a world war, natural disasters, and the worst depression this country has known. They have a resilience born of massive changes—from the tin lizzy to space travel, the five-cent stamp to the Internet, birth control to genetic engineering. Rather than being opposed to change, seniors have been change-agents.

In *Today's Adult,* C. Ferris Jordan describes senior adults as the most diverse group of our population. They have a wide range of interests, physical stamina, activity levels, financial resources, and personalities.[1]

The "Age Wave" Is Here

In his book *Age Wave* Ken Dychtwald popularized the concept that the growing senior adult population is like a tidal wave sweeping across America. If only in terms of sheer numbers, the age wave will change every facet of our society in coming years.[2]

The U.S. Census Bureau's 1990 report is a wake-up call for the church. In 1900 adults 65 or older made up 4% of the population. Americans 85 and older numbered 3.1 million. A child born in 1900 could expect to live to be around 50 years of age.

Since 1900, the number of Americans 65 or older has increased 10 times and the percentage of the population has tripled. They now represent 12.6% of the U.S. population, or about 1 in every 8 Americans. A child born in 1990 can expect to live 75 years.

The 85+ age group had the largest percentage increase of all groups–25 times larger than this age group in 1900. By 2050 their number will approach 18 million, almost 5% of the population.

Geographically, senior adults are concentrated in 9 states, which contain over half (52%) of them. California had 3 million; Florida and New York, 2 million each; and Pennsylvania, Texas, Illinois, Ohio, Michigan, and New Jersey, 1 million each. Some states will experience 100% growth in senior adult population between 1995 and 2020. All other states will experience some increase.

The strain on social services is already being felt in states like Florida and California. The age wave is here. What is your church and community doing to meet the challenges of a rapidly growing senior adult population?

Lifestyle Characteristics

Today's 65 and older seniors are difficult to categorize chronologically. Lifestyle–not age–plays the biggest role in how we minister to them. Here are a few of their lifestyle characteristics.

1. **Marital status**–Half of all older women are widows. There are five times as many widows as widowers. Older men are nearly twice as likely to be married as older women. Although only 5% of seniors are divorced, divorce among older adults has increased 3 times as fast as the older population since 1980.

2. **Living arrangements**–Older Americans are healthier and more independent than their predecessors. Only 5% live in long-term care facilities while 67% live in family settings–either in their own homes or with a relative. The majority live in their own residences. In 1991 42% of older women and 16% of older men lived alone.

3. **Attitudes**–For many of today's seniors, these years are among their most creative and productive. Many reject the stigma that old age means powerlessness and uselessness. They are concerned with maintaining a sense of meaning and purpose for

their lives. As health and mobility decline, some older adults lack a sense of worth. Self-centeredness may result.[3]

4. **Economics**–Persons 65 and older have a median household net worth of $88,634 and a median household income of $20,985. A total of 81% of seniors 65 to 69 are homeowners, while 75% of those 75 and older own homes. Marketing efforts targeting seniors have mushroomed. Publishers of senior-oriented media increased from 279 to 896 from 1988 to 1996.

A Time of Changes and Adjustments

Today's senior adults confront life changes and adjustments on a daily basis. Each senior adult determines for himself or herself whether the changes and adjustments of aging will be positive or negative experiences. Seniors have the opportunity to integrate all of their life experiences to produce a holistic view of their life span, or they can react to aging with despair and disgust.

Robert J. Havinghurst lists six developmental tasks for the later years:

- adjusting to decreasing physical strength and health
- adjusting to retirement and reduced income
- adjusting to death of spouse
- establishing an explicit affiliation with one's own age group
- meeting social and specific obligations
- establishing satisfactory physical living arrangements

The degree to which seniors successfully work through these stages of aging is generally the degree to which they experience the senior years as positive and growth-producing. As we work with today's seniors, we should provide experiences that will lead to the mastery of these developmental tasks.

Impact of Baby Boomer Seniors

Until 1996 the senior adult segment of the U.S. population exhibited slow, steady growth. When baby boomers started turning 50 in

1996, growth began to escalate. As a result of aging boomers, by the year 2030 persons 65 and older will represent 21.8% of the U.S. population.

The most rapid increase in numbers is expected between the years 2010 and 2030 when the last of the baby boom generation reaches age 65. By 2025, the 65+ population will outnumber teenagers by two to one. What a shift from the youth-focused culture of the 1990s!

By 2040 life expectancy will increase to age 86 for men and 91.5 for women. By 2050 the percentage of the U.S. population over the age of 65 will reach 22%. Entire communities—and entire churches—will consist of senior adults.

Lifestyle Characteristics

Generally, boomers have eight characteristics.

1. They prefer short-term projects, short-term studies, and activities that do not call for a long-term commitment. They want easy access to these activities on their time schedules.
2. They are too busy for activities that are not well planned. They will spend their time on organized, quality programming.
3. They will spend money for a good cause—a purpose or benefit they deem worthy.
4. They have grown up with cafeteria-style choices. For the most part loyalty to a particular organization, denomination, or company has not been their style.
5. They are more hands-on than theoretical. They want to experience reality—not just talk or read about it.
6. While still family-oriented, they have experienced a wide variety of family types—from intact nuclear families to single-parent, divorced, and blended families. Family values have been influenced by a society that has devalued the family.
7. Boomers expect to be entertained by televisions, movies, sporting events, VCRs, CDs, computer games, and the Internet.

8. A self-centered—"What's in it for me"—attitude has been their philosophy! They have been called "the me generation" to indicate their self-focus.

Implications for Society

Baby boomers have been individualistic throughout their life spans. Although we do not know exactly what they will be like as senior adults, we can make educated guesses. In *Age Wave* Ken Dychtwald paints the clearest picture of what the age wave will bring.

1. Senior adults will vote more regularly than other groups and make known and promote their viewpoints. Their influence and power will result in political clout heretofore not seen in America. This clout could cause intergenerational conflict over the way our nation's resources are used and distributed.

2. A linear lifestyle will be replaced by cyclic lifestyles. In the past, persons were born, educated, worked, married, raised families, and retired. In the future, major events of our lives will not follow a time or set sequence. Persons will move in and out of the workplace and have multiple careers, marriages, and families.

3. To the new seniors leisure will not mean passive activities. Recreation will include hobbies/crafts, active learning centers, educational seminars, adult sport camps, computers and games, adventure and travel clubs, and time-share lifestyle communities for relaxation and recreation. The key to their choices will be the benefit/value they receive from the activity.

4. Lifelong learning for personal growth and service to others will become the norm. Boomers will participate in self-study programs, lifestyle expeditions (Elder Hostels), academic retirement villages next to colleges and universities, and corporations using older residents for staffing of training centers.

5. Employees will have more control over their lives in the workplace. They will blend: work and leisure; retraining; sabbaticals for education, personal use, and community projects; phased

retirements; part-time work; and part-time retirement. The workplace will reflect a flex place on flex time.

6. Marriage in retirement has already begun to change. The divorce rate for people over the age of 65 is now increasing as rapidly as for younger couples. The number of adults living alone will increase, a fact which affects housing, leisure, and financial services. Participation in clubs, recreational teams, and other social groups which provide companionship will grow accordingly.

7. The family will evolve into a "matrix family"—adult oriented with several generations living together, bound by friendship and choice not blood or obligation. Instead of grown children caring for their aging parents (80% of elderly care), programs that offer care will increase with the use of visiting nurses, in-house health care, care managers who help with medical and social services, and the emergence of adult day care.

8. The maturing marketplace will explode in the years to come. Boomer seniors are in the market for financial services, health, wellness, nutrition products and services, luxury cars, travel and tours, personal care products, second homes, and a wide variety of recreational products and services. America is already realigning products and services to meet their demands.

A Time of Reflection and Service

As boomers enter senior adulthood, the future is bright. They have moved into positions of power and prominence in just about every aspect of American life, transforming it as they take reign.

Boomers are seeking to change the image of senior adulthood, replacing the ageism of a youth-oriented culture with a more positive image of aging. With advances in medicine and technology, this active, vibrant, healthy senior adult population has the potential to bring a mature perspective to social issues facing our nation.

According to Eric Erikson, boomers will desire generativity—the concern with passing along to future generations what one has learned in life—and ego integrity—the achievement of a sense of personal wholeness in life's final stages. These two desires are particularly relevant for church ministries. Churches must tap the wisdom and experience of boomers who want to give back to society knowledge and resources achieved in their lifetimes.

Senior adult leaders who adjust to the new seniors will find them to be a rich source of volunteerism. Helping them achieve their dreams and goals for later years should be a high priority for all senior adult ministries.

Implications for the Church

The boomers have changed every phase of life they have touched, and now they are changing religious institutions. Having grown up in a secularized society with the major upheavals of Vietnam, Watergate, and the sexual revolution, boomers are a study in contrasts.

Some boomers grew up attending worship services, never left the church, and continue active participation. They are strong believers in God, wanting Him personally involved in their lives, and many report being "born-again" evangelicals. Other boomers dropped out of church in their younger years, but have come back. They are "church-hoppers," attending the church with their preferred support groups, singles/senior groups, sports/wellness/recreation, and career-oriented activities. Usually they settle in a large congregation.

Still other boomers have been called "seekers," individualists, operating outside the walls of conventional religion. They merge traditional Judeo-Christian beliefs with other popular ideologies such as astrology, reincarnation, and psychology. They regard all religions as equally worthy. They question church leaders' authority; however, they classify themselves as spiritual. They are more interested in searching for answers than in finding the answer.

You will encounter to some degree all types of boomers as you minister to persons inside and outside your church. Those inclined to organized religion will be reached with innovative programs.

Reaching the seekers will require renewed concentration on evangelism. They represent the greatest number of lost persons. Discipleship will be essential to help them grow spiritually.

Implications for Programming

Thus far we have contrasted today's seniors with the boomer seniors entering senior adulthood. These contrasts provide several implications for the leaders who are responsible for designing and implementing senior adult programming.

1. Continue programs that meet needs and provide services. Today's senior adults are joiners, loyal to their church, tithers, and committed to their communities. Throughout their lives the church has ministered to them through Sunday School, Discipleship Training (BYPU, Training Union, Church Training), senior adult clubs, and social interaction. Church leaders should not stop doing what has worked well with present-day seniors.

2. Expect to provide diversity and options. As persons enter their seniors years, they could potentially participate in senior adult activities for four decades—well into their nineties or for some their hundreds. One type program will not fit all. The church must provide multiple activities, events, programs, and ministries to reach them for Christ and service in His kingdom.

3. Use lifestyles, not age, as the determining factor in ministering to older adults. Reaching them begins with knowing their attitudes and preferences. Avoid stereotyping and typecasting.

4. Involve seniors in mentoring younger age groups. Longer lives and better health will enable them to use their time and energy teaching and training others in such areas as finances, legal issues, marriage and family, and work-related skills.

5. Cultivate their desire for meaning and purpose by providing ministry options which challenge their abilities and interests. Give them God-sized challenges that take them outside the walls of the church to the community and the world.

6. Provide services to seniors in a family context that conveys an attitude of valuing the uniqueness of each individual.
7. Consider the needs of senior adults as you add church staff members. The number of senior adult ministers will increase in coming years while the number of youth ministers will decline.
8. Make outreach to and by senior adults a priority. Prospects for the church increasingly will be unsaved and unchurched seniors.

Implications for Church Facilities

Although seniors in the future will be healthier and more physically fit than today's seniors, they will still feel the effects of the aging process. Church facilities will change to meet their needs.

1. Larger signs will allow for easy reading.
2. Passageways, doors, and other openings will be wider to accommodate walkers and wheelchairs.
3. All areas will be well-lighted.
4. Access to buildings will be on as level a surface as possible. If steps are needed, a ramp will serve as an alternate route. Elevators will be necessities.
5. Handrails will be placed on all stairwells or steps.
6. Parking designated for handicapped and seniors will provide direct access to their areas of the facility.
7. Senior adult areas will be situated near the auditorium.
8. Restrooms will have easy access, wider doors, and more spacious interiors.

Mobilize Senior Adults for Ministry

Many churches are facing a leadership crisis due to several converging factors. The first factor involves the tendency on the part of some senior adults to "retire" from church responsibilities. They feel they have "served their time" and desire to be freed from the strictures of leadership roles. As a result, they are no longer available to fill significant leadership roles they held for many years.

A second factor is the boomer's preference for short-term commitments. Boomers as a group are less institutionally loyal and less likely to sign on for ongoing responsibilities. The third factor involves the baby busters, the "Generation Xers," who have not yet come into their own in leadership roles. A generational conflict exists between the busters and present-day seniors over worship styles.

Recruit Volunteers

You may confront some or all of these issues in your church. If so, the situation raises an interesting set of dynamics. The cause of Christ is mushrooming across our globe, and opportunities for witness abound. In some countries the window of opportunity is now. Our own nation seems ripe for spiritual renewal and awakening.

At the same time, senior adults with the most available time, resources, and experience comprise the fastest growing age group. Is this coincidence? Not according to Dr. Charles Kelley, president of New Orleans Baptist Theological Seminary. In his role as one who prepares young adults for ministry, Dr. Kelley often confronts this issue of a draining leadership pool. He believes senior adults are the answer to the church's leadership woes.

> Two-thirds of the people in the history of the world who have ever lived to the age of 65 are alive today! God has given something to a generation He has not given since the days of Noah: extended life. The age wave is far more than an accident of improvements in medical science or the natural aging process of a large generation. The age wave is one of God's ways to equip His church to fulfill the Great Commission.[4]

To accomplish God's purposes, the church must utilize the resources God provides. God has provided senior adults! Before we can engage this potential source of Kingdom volunteers, we must see them as valuable resources put in our churches "for such a time as this" (Esth. 4:14).

Actively recruit seniors by appealing to their desire to impact the world around them. Prepare to train boomer seniors for service. They will participate in activities for which they feel qualified.

Teach a Biblical View of Aging

The attitude that senior adults are productive and valued leaders is very much a biblical concept. The fact that we are made in the image of God reveals our importance to God (see Gen. 1:27). As we age we do not diminish in our worth to Him or to mankind. The Bible speaks clearly to five beliefs about aging.

1. Aging has purpose and is a normal part of life.

   "There is a time for everything, and a season for every activity under heaven: a time to be born and a time to die" (Eccl. 3:1-2).

2. Seniors deserve our honor, respect, and recognition.

   "'Honor your father and mother'—which is the first command-ment with a promise—'that it may go well with you and that you may enjoy long life on the earth'" (Eph. 6:2-3).

3. Aging provides experience, knowledge, and wisdom, which serve as examples of a worthy life.

   "Is not wisdom found among the aged? Does not long life bring understanding?" (Job 12:12).

4. Senior adults should mentor younger adults.

   "Remember the days of old; consider the generations long past. Ask your father and he will tell you, your elders, and they will explain to you" (Deut. 32:7).

5. God uses people of all ages.

   "'In the last days, God says, I will pour out my Spirit on all peo-ple. Your sons and daughters will prophesy, your young men will see visions, your old men will dream dreams'" (Acts 2:17).

God calls people of all ages in every stage/phase of life to a re-demptive and dynamic relationship with Him. Without it, we are lost and drifting with no direction and meaning to life. All of us should "hunger and thirst for righteousness" (Matt. 5:6). God's redemptive work of grace is given to all for all ages and for all of life.

Cast a New Vision

A wonderful task awaits us as we minister to new generations of senior adults—better educated, healthier, more independent, searching for meaning and purpose. With less emphasis on a linear life span, future seniors will have a mind-set of continued usefulness throughout life. With less emphasis on retirement and more emphasis on lifelong learning and involvement, boomer seniors will look for opportunities to leave a legacy for future generations.

The challenge will not so much be motivating them to serve as it will be influencing their choice to serve in the church. They will have many other options to choose from, including many worthwhile causes. These will compete with the church for a senior's time and attention.

Challenge seniors with a larger vision than adding members or buildings to your church. Challenge them with a kingdom vision of extending the gospel to the unreached neighborhood, community, nation, and world. Once they catch a vision of how their participation serves this larger purpose of Kingdom expansion, opportunities for ministry and service will take on meaning and purpose.

This is our challenge! Shall we mobilize this great army of God and move forward together?

---

[1] C. Ferris Jordan, *Today's Adults: A Profile for Teachers and Leaders* (Nashville: Convention Press, 1993), 9.
[2] Ken Dychtwald, *Age Wave* (New York: Bantam Books, 1990), 21.
[3] Jordan, *Today's Adults: A Profile for Teachers and Leaders*, 9.
[4] Dr. Charles Kelley, conversation with authors, 25 September 1997.

Chapter 2

A Balanced Senior Adult Ministry

by Larry Mizell

The Five Service Areas
Steps to Balancing Your Ministry
Organizing Your Ministry
The Senior Adult Club Concept
A Look Ahead

Ministry with, by, and to senior adults is the goal of senior adult ministry in the local church. Senior adult ministry should meet the needs of all seniors—from those who are very active to those inactive or homebound. It should also be balanced to provide for the spiritual, mental, physical, and social needs of seniors.

In this chapter we will consider ways to balance your ministry and organize it for maximum effectiveness. A flexible approach to organization and activities will allow your senior adult ministry to adapt to younger persons entering senior adulthood.

We are on the threshold of a new era. Traditional ways of ministering no longer suffice. Creative ways of engaging and involving senior adults will emerge. Churches will either prepare for this "age wave" or be swept away by it. Those who prepare will benefit from offering innovative ministries to reach a broad spectrum of seniors.

The Five Service Areas

Jesus is our model of a balanced person who grew spiritually, mentally, relationally, and physically (see Luke 2:52). All of life is to be dedicated to God and used to bring Him glory. Senior adults continue to be growing individuals with a wide range of interests and abilities. Programming for senior adults should be broad-based as well to reflect their diversity in ages, lifestyles, and needs.

Programming should reflect the five service areas of senior adult ministry in the local church. These five areas are:

1. **Spiritual Enrichment**—The need for spiritual growth does not diminish with age. Some seniors are eager to grow in the Lord; others need motivating. Provide resources and activities for continued spiritual growth, such as Sunday morning Bible study, discipleship studies, weekday Bible study, prayer groups and seminars, evangelism training and witnessing, retreats, and state and national conferences for senior adults.

2. **Learning (Growth) Opportunities**—To function in our rapidly-changing world, seniors must continue to learn. Younger seniors have more formal education and will expect the church to offer quality, challenging growth experiences. These would include seminars and workshops held at or sponsored by their churches.

3. **Socialization**—Seniors enjoy parties, banquets, trips, leisure activities, dinner clubs, recreation, club meetings, and rallies. Socialization activities meet friendship needs and provide biblical *koinonia*. Each social activity should have a spiritual component. Fellowship and recreation events provide a non-threatening opportunity to reach and disciple unchurched and unsaved seniors.

4. **Services Needed**—A small percentage of seniors need services your church can provide, such as meals-on-wheels; transportation; homebound ministry; telephone reassurance; home repairs; and day-care to name a few. Determine the needs in your local situation and supply them as God gives the workers.

5. **Services Provided**—The flip side of needing services is providing services. After determining the services needed, plan ministry projects to address them. Remember that seniors themselves are a capable pool of volunteers for ministry. Many of them have

the time, resources, health, and motivation to significantly impact their churches, communities, and world for Christ.

Plans made by and with seniors have a greater success rate. Allow senior adults to take responsibility for their own programming.

A Balanced Ministry

As a leader of senior adults in your church, you may be involved in one, several, or most of the senior adult program and ministry areas. Perhaps you are a Sunday School teacher but do not sing in the senior adult choir. Or perhaps you participate in the recreation program, but you have never been on a mission trip abroad.

This book has been designed to help you visualize how the different components of senior adult ministry fit together to achieve several important objectives.

- provide balance so that seniors are encouraged to grow spiritually, relationally, mentally, and physically
- maintain distinctives so that one program area of the church does not overlap or replace another vital area
- meets needs which might otherwise go unattended
- provide variety to attract a diversity of senior adults
- challenge seniors to meaningful volunteer and leadership roles

Read each chapter–especially those unrelated to your area of expertise or interest! Grow in your understanding of how each area can expand and energize your senior adult ministry. Read with a "can-do" attitude. We believe the ideas are adaptable for any size church, in any location, with an organization tailored to your particular needs and interests.

Remember that specific programs for your church have to be just that. They must be specifically geared to meet the interests and needs of your seniors—not just copied from another church.

As you read, use the margins to jot down possibilities for your church. Then use the leader guide on pages 220-221 to review key concepts with other senior adult leaders in your church.

A Balanced Target Audience

A balanced senior adult ministry includes a balanced target audience. Seniors have lifestyle differences. Horace L. Kerr gave a clear picture of the social and physical needs of senior adults based on their activity levels.

# Relative Needs by Activity Level Total Population Age 60+	
Go-Go 15%	
Will-Go 35%	**Social Needs**
Slow-Go 35%	
No-Go 10%	**Physical Needs**
Can't Go 5% (Institutional)	

Some seniors are ready to go anywhere and participate in most anything. Others are beginning to slow down. Seniors may come to one meeting or event per week or go on an overnight trip once or twice a year. Others do not participate at all; some are institutionalized. A balanced program will reach all five senior lifestyles–the go-go, the will-go, the slow-go, the no-go, and the can't go.

These five lifestyles are unrelated to age. Do not assume that an 80-year-old is a no-goer and a 60-year-old is a go-goer. Lifestyle is a factor of physical, emotional, and spiritual health; finances; personal interests and choices; and perceived social needs. Approach programming based on lifestyles and not ages.

Think of specific seniors in your church that represent these five lifestyles. As you develop a well-rounded ministry with, by, and to senior adults, take into consideration the stages of activity and provide for all of them.

Steps to Balancing Your Ministry

Adequate, accurate planning allows for a smooth-running senior adult ministry. The following steps will help you begin/maintain a balanced senior adult ministry.

1. **Recognize the need for a coordinated senior adult ministry in your church.** Perhaps you have several senior adult program areas or through-the-week ministries which operate fairly independently of each other. A coordinated ministry brings each of these together under one "umbrella" so that each functions effectively. Bring the need for coordination to the attention of your pastor, other key leaders, and the congregation.

2. **Select a coordinator of senior adult ministries.** With pastoral backing and church approval, seek a person—either staff or volunteer—to coordinate the total ministry.

3. **Form a task force.** The coordinator should enlist a task force with the help of the pastor, church council, or the appropriate church committee. Members of the task force should represent the senior areas in Sunday School, Discipleship Training, music, recreation, missions, and the senior adult club if you have one. Include others on the task force who would like to be involved and could contribute to the overall planning.

4. **Use a strategy-planning process to assess your current ministry and plan for the future.** This process is outlined in chapter

11 and can be modified to fit the needs of your church. It includes such actions as profiling the senior adults in your church and community, surveying to discover senior adult interests and needs, identifying available resources in your church and community, determining priority issues and concerns, and formulating objectives for your ministry. The strategy planning document then becomes the foundation for your ministry.

5. **Suggest ways to strengthen existing ministries.** What you are presently offering seniors in your church meets needs and produces growth in individuals. Any organization can be more effective. Encourage the task force to make recommendations to strengthen existing church organizations such as Sunday School, Discipleship Training, music, and missions groups.

6. **Elect an on-going senior adult steering committee.** Task force members can become the basis for a Senior Adult Ministry Council (SAMC), whose stated purpose is to provide coordination. The senior adult minister/coordinator serves as SAMC president and members represent all church organizations, church staff, and major programs and ministries developed to implement your vision of senior adult ministry. Members of the steering committee can serve one-year or rotating terms. In some cases, persons serve as long as they hold certain positions in the program area they represent (senior adult Sunday School director, senior adult choir president, and so on).

Organizing Your Ministry

Senior adult ministry (SAM) can be organized using a variety of models. The chart on the next page pictures a possible organization of the SAMC. This organizational model recognizes that SAM is under the umbrella of the church and must fit its overall purpose and direction. Adapt this structure to your church. This model works for small and large churches—those with a simple organizational structure and those with multiple programs and activities.

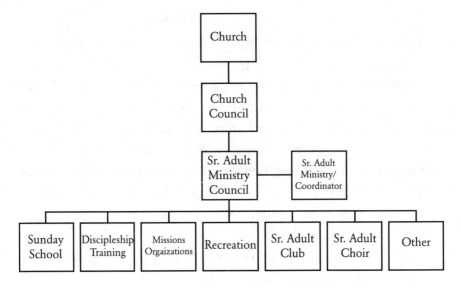

For churches that have a church council in place, SAMC provides a representative to reflect the needs and interests of seniors. For churches that do not have a church council, SAMC is a standing committee which relates to the pastor or another staff person.

Each program or activity of SAM is represented on the council. The council may also include "floating" members not identified with a particular area. The council should reflect the interests and diversity of all ages and lifestyles of seniors.

With an organization in place, begin scheduling activities and developing new programs and ministries. The council should meet annually for planning. The monthly council meeting allows time to add, delete, and adjust programs and ministries as needed to ensure quality activities and structure.

Always calendar SAM activities in coordination with the church-wide calendar. Enlist the help of the SAMC to promote churchwide events to senior adults.

The Senior Adult Club Concept

Many churches have senior adult clubs as part of a total senior adult ministry. Club activities serve as the hub of through-the-week activities. Senior adult clubs have been popular vehicles for meeting needs of seniors for the past 30 years.

With baby boomers entering senior adulthood beginning in 1996, churches should rethink the club concept to determine if it meets the needs of younger seniors. Boomers tend to be interested in short-term commitments that bring immediate results. They are not "joiners" in the traditional use of the word. Clubs may not attract them to the extent they have attracted older seniors.

Your SAMC may determine to offer more than one club or allow the club to meet the needs of older seniors without inferring that younger seniors must participate. One Texas church identifies its senior adult club as "Forerunners." Because of lifestyle and age differences, club activities are promoted for "Rookies" (55-64), "Veterans" (65-74), and "Hall of Famers" (75+). Different strategies are used to attract each group.

The basic club organization requires a president, vice-president, and secretary/treasurer. The officers and committee chairpersons serve as the planning council for the club. Remember that the more people who assume responsibility, the more participation you will have and the lighter the load will be on those who lead. Divide the workload among as many people as possible. Here are the duties of the officers:

President—Works closely with the senior adult minister/coordinator, serves as the club representative on the SAMC, presides over club meetings and club council meetings, and appoints special committees as needed.

Vice-president—Works closely with the club president and presides in his/her absence, serves as chairperson of committee enlistment, organizes the club members into groups for telephoning, and assists the president in appointing special committees.

Secretary—Takes minutes of club council meetings, keeps an active membership roll, registers attendees, keeps scrapbook of activities, enlists greeters for special events, and prepares the club yearbook.

Committee chairpersons, who are appointed to carry out the activities of the club, include the following:

Program Committee—Plans the programs for general club meetings and assists the president in planning special programs and events.

Social Committee—Plans club socials, fellowships, and parties.

Publicity Committee—Publicizes club programs, meetings, and events in all media available, including the church newsletter, senior adult newsletter, local radio and television, and newspapers.

Benevolence Committee—Keeps the club aware of needs of bereaved persons and organizes response with food or other assistance as needed (in cooperation with the total church).

Hospitality Committee—Makes all the arrangements for food at meetings and all special occasions.

Decorations Committee—Decorates for all meetings of the club and other events as planned.

Greeting Committee—Welcomes members and guests to all functions and follows-up on guests to reach them for Christ and the church.

A Look Ahead

Follow the steps to planning an effective and fulfilling ministry with, by, and to senior adults. Balance it by considering the spiritual, educational, social, recreational, and ministry needs of seniors. Consider seniors who are active as well as those who have begun to slow down or cannot participate.

Visualize a future characterized by seniors who are active, healthy, mobile, and motivated to make a difference in their world. Plan with the needs of unsaved and unreached seniors in mind. Challenge your seniors with the words of Jeremiah: "'For I know the plans I have for you,' declares the Lord, 'plans to prosper you and not to harm you, plans to give you hope and a future'" (Jer. 29:11).

Chapter 3

Life-Changing Bible Study

by David Apple

Reaching Senior Adults for Bible Study
Teaching Senior Adults
Involving Senior Adults in Bible Study
Organizing Principles for Life-Changing Bible Study
Targeting Senior Adults
Providing Weekday and Special Event Bible Studies

The Bible Teaching and Reaching organization (the Sunday School) of a church serves as the hub of ministries impacting senior adults. It is the hub because:

- The life-changing Word of God is the textbook for believers and the basis of every church program and ministry.
- Sunday School is the Bible teaching, caring, evangelistic, and fellowship arm of the church.
- Sunday School has the largest group of senior adult members and prospects.
- Sunday School identifies potential church leaders.
- Every other ministry/organization of a church should be an outgrowth of intentionally applying God's Word.

A church that wants to strengthen its ministry to senior adults will give priority to Bible study. Whether you call it Sunday School, Bible study, cell groups, or another name, the study of God's Word is the centerpiece of ministry with senior adults. In this chapter we will consider the challenges of reaching and teaching those just entering senior adulthood as well as present members and prospects.

Reaching Senior Adults for Bible Study

During previous decades, senior adults were often grouped into one general category. Although senior adults have always had distinctive needs and developmental tasks, those now entering the senior adult years refuse to be the target of stereotypes.

Consider a brief list describing the diversity of senior adults:

- Although many are Christians, most seniors are non-Christians. They have no relationship with any group of believers for Bible study, Christian support, encouragement, ministry, or discipleship.
- Many churched seniors are reassessing their ministry and leadership roles. Some are opting to "retire" from church responsibilities. Others are willing to take on more roles.
- Although many are now single, most were married and still think of themselves as married adults; others are married.
- Some have grown children, school-aged children, or in exceptional cases preschoolers while others have no children.
- Educational levels may vary from a grade-school education to advanced degrees; many seniors are attending a college or trade school; others pursue continuing education classes.
- Most senior adults are retired from employment (some have retired several times); however, many are working part-time or volunteering their time to help others.
- Many are living at home; others are being cared for by relatives; and a small percentage are cared for in public or private facilities.
- A majority of caregivers for the elderly are themselves senior adults.

Traditionally senior adults have been grouped for Bible study by age and gender. In our complex society, age is no longer the lone determiner of lifestyle. A 60-year-old man may be in his first career, second or third career, retired, or a student. He may be a grandfather or have children in high school. He may be in a long-term marriage, a second or third marriage, divorced or never-married. He may be a mature Christian or a new believer. He may be accustomed to a coed class rather than a men's class.

Because of the active lifestyle of today's seniors, Bible study competes for their attention just as it does for the attention of younger generations. Older seniors grew up in a culture where the Bible was read at home, studied as literature in schools, and quoted in public addresses. Today seniors rarely see or hear the Bible referenced in daily life. Unless they have cultivated the personal discipline of regular Bible study, they will find other activities to fill their days.

Seniors have unlimited opportunities for learning through the media, computers, continuing education classes, and printed resources. Many are searching for experiences that stress purpose and meaning. No longer can we assume senior adults will just come to Sunday School by habit or conviction.

Younger Seniors

First, let's consider the challenge of reaching the Baby Boomer seniors who began turning 50 in 1996. Younger seniors are unlikely to identify with older senior adults. Younger seniors are churched, unchurched, and lost adults.

1. Churched—When adults become empty nesters, they lose one of the powerful motivators for attending Sunday School—taking their children. Some empty nesters drop out of Sunday School. Others drop out or attend infrequently because they are grouped with persons much older or in different lifestyles from their own. In some churches, a younger senior could be in class with his or her parent because of promotion to the one senior adult department.

Other seniors who travel extensively or spend weekends at another location drop out because they do not want to be considered "bad" class members or receive absentee calls or notes. Still others become dropouts due to divorce or death of a spouse, especially if they have been in a coed class.

Churches must be willing to take into account the lifestyle differences and preferences of younger seniors and promote a learning environment that accommodates their needs. Leaders must create new classes, provide dynamic and creative learning experiences, and encourage fellowship and belonging without alienating those who cannot or will not attend weekly.

2. Unchurched—Adults who have never cultivated the habit of regular Sunday School attendance can be reached as they enter the senior years through innovative strategies that engage their interest in a particular ministry, social, or recreational activity.

Churches must offer special events targeted to younger seniors with the view of cultivating them for regular Bible study. Short-term missions can be the catalyst that sparks serious study of God's Word. (See p. 117 for ideas for mission involvement.) Often a recreational activity or trip will build friendships that lead to Sunday School attendance. (See pp. 142-147 for recreational ideas that promote outreach.)

3. Lost—Unchurched and lost younger seniors can be found in health clubs, social and community organizations, on committees, and in board rooms. Encourage churched seniors to identify neighbors, coworkers, and friends who need to know Christ. Actively cultivate those persons. Train Sunday School outreach teams in how to effectively present a Christian witness.

Provide entry points sponsored by the church where unsaved adults can become acquainted with members as well as ministries of the church. Guest speakers, Bible conferences, ministry fairs, or other age-group or churchwide events provide opportunities for members to invite others to "check out" the church. Poll unreached adults about topics and interests they would like to study. Initiate Bible study groups that meet away from the church and/or at other times than Sunday morning. These groups and events will serve as entry points only to the degree that you follow-up with demonstrations of care and concern.

Many younger seniors have the time, expertise, and resources to participate in community ministries, such as building a house, feeding and housing the homeless, or providing a food bank. Their interest may be humanitarian; however, association with Christians can lead to an interest in Christ, who motivates the ministry. (See pp. 86-90 and 156-157 for ideas on service projects that can attract lost or unchurched seniors.)

Middle and Older Seniors

Although middle and older seniors may be more likely to identify with senior adult activities, they may be nominally involved in Sunday School. Let's look at some reasons they are difficult to involve in life-changing Bible study.

1. Churched—Generally active members acknowledge the need for systematic Bible study through the Sunday School. However, by the time they reach the senior years many of them assume a comfortable familiarity with the Bible. Sunday School is more a time to rehash Bible truths they learned many years ago than a time for new insights.

Although many seniors are serious students of the Bible, they may focus on Bible knowledge which does not necessarily translate into developing godly character. They may have made God's Word something to be studied more than to be applied. They have not caught the life-transforming message from God.

Although some seniors are limited by health and transportation, many do not attend regular Bible study out of the mistaken notion that they have "arrived" spiritually. Seniors need to view Bible study as integral to growing in Christlikeness—a lifelong process. They need to set and work toward goals in Christian character, attitude, and action. Those who teach seniors need to view this age group as still becoming all they were called to be in Christ.

The Scripture "is living and active. Sharper than any double-edged sword, it penetrates even to dividing soul and spirit, joints and marrow; it judges the thoughts and attitudes of the heart" (Heb. 4:12). When we have truly incorporated the message of the Bible into our lives, we can never remain the same. Churches must provide Bible study that encourages continued spiritual growth throughout every stage of life.

2. Unchurched—Unchurched senior adults are one of the church's largest mission fields. Some from this group were once active in church. For many reasons—dissatisfaction or disillusionment with the church, shift or Sunday work schedules, family difficulties, or personal sin—they have strayed away from the church. Bible study is a natural and direct opportunity for the church to reclaim them as active members. Every senior adult Bible study class should maintain a list of prospects for Bible study.

Other seniors have never been a part of a church. As they grow older, they naturally think more about death and eternity. The church may find a receptivity that was not present in their youth or middle age.

As we think of the unreached people groups of our nation, we must include the senior adults among the immigrant population. Seniors are found among the wealthy, the poor, racial and cultural groups, members of cults and sects, and our neighbors. Consider the neighbor down the street whose car never leaves the driveway on Sunday morning. The unchurched are all around us.

Think of the places you see senior adults: senior or community centers; golf courses; post offices; grocery stores; gas stations; walking; or volunteering in hospitals, libraries, and community ministries. Seniors are generally willing to talk—even to strangers. Engage them in conversation. Ask them if they attend a regular Bible study. Keep in mind that most senior adults are NOT in Bible study and the senior years are ripe for a focus on spiritual issues.

3. Lost—The fields are ripe for harvest with older adults in our communities who do not know Jesus as their Savior. Certainly, those of us who see them as lost and in danger of eternal separation from God should be challenged to reach out to them with the message of everlasting life. Many from this age group acknowledge a belief in God—even belief in angels and prayer. However, when pressed about a personal relationship with God through Jesus Christ, they cannot relate to the term "born again."

The FAITH Evangelism Strategy has boldly emphasized evangelism through the Sunday School. Sunday School has traditionally been identified as the main soul-winning arm of the church. Many churches that have implemented the FAITH strategy have seen unsaved senior adults come to faith in Christ and nurtured them through the Sunday School. Contact your state convention's Sunday School Department for information about the FAITH strategy.

Teaching Senior Adults

In order to attract the inactive, unchurched, and lost seniors in our society, Bible study must be a meaningful, life-changing experience. Often, Bible study classes are assumed to be boring lectures or superficial discussions. What a contrast to the experience of the early believers! Their lives were literally turned upside down by the message of the gospel (see Acts 17:6).

Acts 2:41-47 identifies some significant characteristics of those whose lives were revolutionized by the gospel. As you read it, underline key actions that identify a dynamic group experience.

> Those who accepted his message were baptized, and about three thousand were added to their number that day. They devoted themselves to the apostles' teaching and to the fellowship, to the breaking of bread and to prayer. Everyone was filled with awe, and many wonders and miraculous signs were done by the apostles. All the believers were together and had everything in common. Selling their possessions and goods, they gave to anyone as he had need. Every day they continued to meet

together in the temple courts. They broke bread in their homes and ate together with glad and sincere hearts, praising God and enjoying the favor of all the people. And the Lord added to their number daily those who were being saved.

Life-changing encounters with God's Word (steadfast in the apostles' doctrine) affected every aspect of the new believers' lives. Review the list of actions you underlined from the passage.

Your list probably included such actions as: prayer, caring, praise, fellowship, evangelism, and community involvement. A class that focuses only on covering Bible lessons without intentionally relating God's Word to life becomes self-absorbed and loses its purpose. A class focused on relating God's Word to life and involving/impacting others will produce the same types of results described in Acts 2:41-47.

Life-changing Bible study is the exciting, dynamic interchange between God's Word and life—no matter how simple or complicated life is, no matter how much joy or sorrow surrounds life, no matter what questions have been raised. Life-changing Bible study answers the question, How does the message of God's Word relate personally to each life experience or concern?

Churches have the opportunity and responsibility of leading senior adults to intersect their lives with the unchanging and LIFE-CHANGING message of God's Word. Read the passages below:

My word that goes out from my mouth...will not return to me empty, but will accomplish what I desire and achieve the purpose for which I sent it (Isa. 55:11).
Continue in what you have learned and have become convinced of, because you know those from whom you learned it, and how from infancy you have known the holy Scriptures, which are able to make you wise for

salvation through faith in Christ Jesus. All Scripture is God-breathed and is useful for teaching, rebuking, correcting and training in righteousness, so that the man of God may be thoroughly equipped for every good work (2 Tim. 3:14-17).

Then Jesus came to them and said, "All authority in heaven and on earth has been given to me. Therefore go and make disciples of all nations, baptizing them in the name of the Father and of the Son and of the Holy Spirit, and teaching them to obey everything I have commanded you. And surely I am with you always, to the very end of the age" (Matt. 28:18-20).

These representative passages challenge us to consider the privilege and responsibility of teaching and applying God's Word.

The paragraphs that follow focus on how to group, schedule, and teach the Bible so that younger seniors as well as older seniors will discover the life-changing message of God's Word. Share this information with each senior adult Sunday School leader and teacher.

Involving Senior Adults in Bible Study

What is the purpose and role of a Bible teacher? The biblical role of the teacher is best understood as that of a disciple-maker. A good teacher helps create or develop learners—persons who want to discover more about the truths of God's Word and how His Word applies to their lives.

Some teachers feel they have to cover all the elements given in the teacher's quarterly for a particular lesson; if they fail to do so, they have not taught the lesson. The needs and concerns of class members are secondary and may be missed completely in the classroom experience. Teachers should be guides, leading participants through experiences that help them discover truths, understand the biblical content, and apply that content to daily living. The following suggestions will enable a senior adult teacher to become a disciple-maker.

Provide an atmosphere conducive to learning—Surroundings play an important role in effective learning. Here are some suggestions for improving the learning environment for senior adults. As you read through the list, underline suggestions you feel would improve the quality of Bible study in your class:

- Older seniors may expect the teacher to lecture from behind a podium. Younger seniors expect the teacher to sit as a part of the group. The informal environment encourages more freedom of expression as learners relate to the Bible truths, to the teacher, and to each other.
- Members should sit where they can see one another and the teacher. Chairs should be positioned in a semicircle facing a focal wall. A chalkboard or large sheets of paper, posters, and other appropriately sized teaching items should be used near or attached to this wall.
- Remove visuals on the walls that do not relate to the current unit and lesson. Visuals can be placed in the room before the session and revealed or uncovered at the appropriate time in the lesson. Then take them down after the lesson if other groups will be using the room.
- Good lighting, a moderate room temperature, comfortable chairs, and pleasant smells are very important. Secure items that will adjust or improve the environment, such as a small heater or fan, lamps, or cushions for chairs.

While the physical arrangement of the room is important, an atmosphere of fellowship and concern is much more important. If members and prospects do not feel welcome, part of the class, and accepted as contributors in learning, learning will be minimized. Consider these suggestions for ways to provide an atmosphere of fellowship and concern.

- Greet members and others warmly and by name.
- Get to know every member and prospect. Provide opportunities for them to express their needs and concerns. As you prepare for Sunday's class session, plan what you will say in relation to these needs.
- Lead members to use the spiritual gift(s) God has given them. These gifts will enhance the Bible study as you call on members to respond in ways that match their gifts (take a plant to a sick member, mentor a new Christian, lead a nursing home service, and so on).

Involve learners in appropriate learning experiences—Remember that participation is not limited to verbal responses. A teacher who uses speaking, writing, reading, hearing, and thinking activities increases the likelihood that learning will be retained and applied to life.

Planning to involve members means selecting methods and activities that will be appropriate to the target group and to learning styles. Some seniors prefer to write answers to questions on a worksheet while others prefer to verbalize their responses. Some are more comfortable expressing themselves artistically or through poems or music. Encourage verbal participation, but do not put anyone in an uncomfortable position in front of a group.

Encourage learners to bring their Bibles and underline verses or make notes in the margins. Provide commentary materials for persons who might want to do additional research. Various Bible translations offer a broader understanding of the meaning of a Bible word or passage. Seniors appreciate the clarity brought by comparing translations, commentaries, and experiences.

Selected resources, including *Biblical Illustrator*, are designed particularly for providing in-depth Bible background study. Although these resources often are used only by teachers, many seniors would find these resources particularly appealing sources of new information.

Members of the class are also resources. They possess pictures, slides, coins, artifacts, books and articles and other memorabilia from trips to Bible lands and other life experiences.

Using Variety in Teaching and Learning Experiences
- helps maintain interest
- takes advantage of different learning styles
- provides opportunities and freedom to participate
- encourages silent members to get involved
- increases the chances of learning
- encourages teacher-member interaction

Use Teaching Methods Effectively—The following teaching methods have been proven to work effectively with senior adults. The only way to become comfortable using them is to use them over and over.

1. Brainstorming—There are three primary actions in brainstorming. First, state the problem and ask for ideas. Encourage learners to respond freely and without fear. Record or designate someone to record every response on the chalkboard or large sheet of paper. Do not evaluate responses. Every response is accepted and written. The activity continues until ideas are exhausted.

Second, evaluate the ideas. Rank them or check the most appropriate. Third, encourage members to implement one or more.

2. Case Study—A case study is an account of a life situation that presents a real or hypothetical problem. Enough details are included for group members to be able to analyze the situation and suggest possible solutions. Or, members may be asked to evaluate the solution given.

Frequently case studies are presented in the lesson commentary or teaching suggestions. Teachers should adapt these case studies to fit the particular circumstances or needs of members in their class or people in their community.

Consider asking members to write the case study. Avoid use of actual (personal) situations known to learners. The risk of embarrassment or breaking of confidence is too great.

3. Discussion—Guided group discussion allows members to share ideas freely. Learners are encouraged to express their opinions and relate information in an informal atmosphere. Discussion can be a powerful tool for creating cohesiveness in a group as members have opportunity to interact and react to one another.

Arrange the chairs so that participants can make eye contact. Encourage honest response. Monitor the direction of the discussion to keep it focused on the topic. Seek to involve all learners.

4. Small groups or buzz groups—Divide the class into small groups (usually 3-5 people). Determine the number of groups by the class size. Consider your class before asking senior adults to move across the room. Those with physical limitations may prefer talking with those nearest to where they are sitting.

Make definite small-group assignments and set a time limit for discussion. Suggest that a recorder report the group's discussion to the entire class. Provide appropriate resources for small group use, such as a notepad and pen, tear sheet or posterboard, and markers. Allow adequate time for reports from each group.

5. Mini-Lecture—A mini-lecture is a short planned talk on a chosen subject for the purpose of instruction. The objective is to give the learner specific information that he or she would not otherwise have. Consider using a mini-lecture when time is limited or when the leader is the only one with the needed information.

A good presentation must be planned and well-organized. The teacher must become very familiar with the material, preferably presenting the material without reading it to the class. Appropriate visuals reinforce the presentation. For maximum involvement, give listening teams an assignment before the mini-lecture; then, allow time for teams to briefly meet to discuss their assignment. Call for reports.

6. Question and Answer–This method allows leader and learners to ask questions and receive responses about a stated topic. The purpose of this method is to acquire or clarify information.

Closed questions have a definite, provable answer and are used to review material presented from the Bible or study materials. Open questions call for reflection and analysis and may have a variety of answers. Open questions evaluate or lead to self-evaluation.

7. Introduce Creative Teaching Methods–Optional or more creative teaching methods include combinations of the basic methods plus methods such as the following:

Listening or Observing Methods:

Stories	Audio Recordings
Quotations	Resource Persons
Statistics	Object Lessons
Poetry	Filmstrips, Video, other electronics

Writing Methods:

Worksheets	Note taking
Outlines	Word studies
Attitude scales	Opinionnaires
Creative writing	Paraphrasing Scripture
Open-ended sentences	

Verbal Methods:

Reading aloud	Interview
Listening teams	Debate/Panel
Assignment/report	Personal sharing/testimony
Drama/monologue/role play	

Use appropriate learning aids–Teaching aids are included in the teaching packets available for the dated adult Bible study curriculum series provided by LifeWay Christian Resources. The packets include items to be used by the teacher as well as members.

Packets include colorful unit and theme posters, maps, and reproducible items such as questionnaires, research assignments, and various other materials and activities. Although every resource item will not be appropriate for seniors, teachers can easily customize ideas and suggestions provided in these teaching helps.

Teachers also can prepare their own teaching aids. Many ideas are suggested and illustrated in teacher quarterlies. Teaching aids must be appropriate for older members—large enough to be read or seen with little shading. Use contrasting colors. If you choose to use cassette tapes or other audio or visual material, make sure you will not be disturbing other classes.

The Sunday School curriculum materials published by LifeWay Christian Resources of the Southern Baptist Convention are designed to help you study and teach God's Word. Call 1-800-458-2772 to order or inquire about resources. Also, feel free to write to share comments or receive special help regarding curriculum materials or ministry concerns. Write to: Adult Biblical Studies, MSN 175, 127 Ninth Avenue, North, Nashville, Tennessee 37234.

Organizing Principles for Life-Changing Bible Study

Every Bible study class needs an organization in place that enables it to effectively reach, teach, minister, fellowship, and worship together. Younger seniors need the freedom to develop an organization that uniquely meets the needs of the targeted group.

Assign job responsibilities to leaders of each class. The titles of leaders are flexible and can be customized by a class or church. Likewise, many classes will need to combine responsibilities. The basic organization suggests a teacher and leaders for care groups, outreach-evangelism, ministry teams, fellowship and prayer. (Responsibilities of care groups and ministry teams are covered in pp. 83-85.) A secretary keeps a current membership roll and checks it each week.

In some churches a team of teachers work together in each class. Team teachers lead short-term assignments. This arrangement could be appropriate for working as well as retired seniors who may not be able or willing to commit to a year or more assignment because of travel or family responsibilities. One person is to be ultimately accountable for the work of the class.

The following **principles** relate directly to organizing Bible study opportunities with senior adults.

1. The ideal size of a Bible study class for senior adults is between 10-15 persons present. To achieve this average attendance, cultivate an enrollment of twice the anticipated average attendance.
2. Although many factors impact average attendance (health and mobility, transportation to and from class, extreme weather conditions) attendance is directly correlated to the enrollment. When the enrollment goes up, attendance goes up. Attendance is also impacted by the number and quality of weekly contacts members and prospects have from leaders and other members.
3. In order to increase average attendance, adult Bible study classes need to actively cultivate at least as many prospective members as they have persons enrolled in the class.
4. Classes generally reach their maximum size in 12-18 months.
5. Unless there are intentional strategies for adding more people than are departing, the class size will soon plateau or dwindle.
6. New classes should be added when classes reach their maximum.
7. Some churches with multiple classes for senior adults organize into departments to coordinate the ministry of up to six classes.
8. The chosen organizational method must be evaluated in terms of communication (How easy is it for newcomers to understand and become a part of the existing structure?), time (Does maintaining the organization take up time needed for Bible study?) and effectiveness (Does the organization result in reaching, teaching, ministering, praying, fellowshipping, and worshiping?).

Targeting Senior Adults

Instead of only relying on the traditional grouping of seniors by age and gender, try groupings based on targeting specific senior lifestyles, geographic locations, time and day of the week, and teaching approach. "Targeting" in no way seeks to eliminate persons or groups from Bible study. On the other hand, targeting helps a class focus on relating to specific groups of unchurched seniors.

Targeting by Lifestyle

Some churches group adults according to marital status. Now churches are experimenting with classes based on the ages of a couple's children or grandchildren. Persons who have teenagers might have more in common with each other than persons grouped simply because they are 50 years old. Some senior adult men have preschoolers! Others have their first grandchild or a grandchild graduating from college.

Another lifestyle grouping applies to work. Those who are no longer employed full-time are placed in class together, while those who are still working or working part-time are in other classes.

Targeting by Location

Bible study classes are being held in homes, businesses, and clubhouses. Multi-unit housing, nursing homes, retirement homes, and community centers are sites for studying God's Word. In Southern states where "snowbirds" gather for the winter, Bible studies are held in mobile home parks and recreational facilities. Reaching unchurched seniors will require moving Bible study away from the church and into locations where seniors live, work, or play.

Many churches are familiar with the Adults Away ministry, which was designed originally for Sunday School classes to keep up with and minister to military personnel, college students, institutionalized persons and missionaries. Churches are learning to utilize Adults Away approaches for senior adults who travel or move away for part of the year. Request free material on starting or strengthening Adults Away ministries by contacting your Baptist association or state convention's Sunday School office.

Although a fairly new vehicle for many senior adults, the Internet is becoming a well-received approach for interacting with others. Electronic mail and "chat rooms" give an increasing number of senior adults a wide variety of opportunities for discussing spiritual issues and needs. Churches with web sites can both publicize and provide Bible studies to net users in their own homes.

Targeting by Time/Day

Sunday morning continues to be the best time in most settings for the church to sponsor Bible classes. Most churched seniors set time aside on Sunday morning to be in a Bible study group. Many unchurched senior adults acknowledge Sunday as an appropriate day for Bible study and worship.

However, Bible study can occur any time during the day and on any day. With our 24-hour-a-day society, many older workers are not available on Sundays. Providing other Bible study options gives opportunities they would miss if Sunday were the only option.

Some churches have tried Saturday night church in an attempt to attract Sunday workers and those who would otherwise be unavailable. Services usually include a variety of Bible study options, as well as a traditional or contemporary worship experience.

Targeting by Teaching Approach

Today's seniors often respond well to lecture but enjoy the close fellowship of a classroom setting. Others prefer a discussion format.

Younger seniors are more independent learners. Many of them prefer a teacher who guides the learning experience. They want the freedom to give input to the lesson. Offering more than one type of study approach will attract more seniors.

Some may prefer the anonymity of a large class that is nonparticipatory. The class may be taught by a Bible scholar or use materials on film or videotape. A pastor's auditorium class appeals to those who do not desire personal interaction.

Many adults who cannot or will not participate in a classroom are approachable one-on-one. Materials normally used in a home-bound ministry can be adapted for use with individuals who are not open to studying in a group. (See p. 49 for resources.)

Targeting by Language/Culture

Many communities are experiencing an influx of immigrants with language and cultural differences. Senior adults often move to this country as part of an extended family. Bible study classes in their native languages or that consider cultural differences open the door to ministering. Baptist associations and state convention offices have information on how to begin ethnic ministries, including how to obtain Bibles in other languages. The Bible is often used as a text in basic English classes sponsored by churches.

Targeting by Affinity

Persons who share a similar interest, hobby, job skill, background, or sport can be targeted for Bible study groups. The possibilities are endless. For example, motorcycle groups around our nation take weekend trips together that include Bible study and worship services at campsites. Campers, hikers, climbers, those who follow the racing circuit, and entertainers group together for Bible study. Affinity works well for Bible studies in the workplace.

Targeting by Intergenerational Groupings

Some churches offer short-term intergenerational Bible studies where participants are grouped by "families" made up of persons from each age group and not necessarily by family relationship. Thus, for Bible study a "family" would have a combination of one or more preschoolers, children, teenagers, younger adults and older adults. Some churches use this approach as a summer option or during a special churchwide emphasis. (For a list of intergenerational resource materials, see p. 167.)

Diversity in grouping, setting, and teaching/learning style offers new avenues for reaching people. By creatively offering options that are attractive to younger seniors, they will find their place in the Bible Teaching and Reaching program of the church.

Providing Weekday and Special Event Bible Studies

Seniors need more than one opportunity a week to study God's Word with other believers. Here are ideas for additional studies:

Weekday Bible Studies

Weekday Bible studies appeal to those who cannot attend on Sunday mornings, those who work with other age groups on Sundays, and those who desire additional Bible study opportunities. They provide an excellent opportunity for inviting unsaved or unchurched friends and neighbors to attend.

Have the studies on a publicized schedule, either weekly or monthly. If possible, arrange them during the noon hour so that those who are employed or cannot drive at night can attend.

If a meal is included, try a variety of menus and keep the cost low. Some groups bring covered dishes or sack lunches and others meet in the banquet rooms of restaurants.

Topics for weekday Bible studies are unlimited. Topical or book studies are popular. Teachers are generally selected for their knowledge in a particular area and donate their time.

Adult Vacation Bible School

Many seniors have fond memories of attending Vacation Bible School as a child. They have taught or helped with VBS for their children. Now they can enjoy a VBS designed just for them.

Select dates and times that correspond to your church's VBS or choose another time appropriate to your senior adults. Allow 3 to 5 days. You will need 2 hours for the study and an additional 40-45 minutes if you include crafts.

LifeWay Christian Resources publishes a VBS curriculum for adults each year. In addition to a Bible study, the materials include a theme, publicity, arts and crafts, recreation and visual aids.

Homebound Ministry

Homebound ministry targets persons of all ages who cannot physically attend Sunday School on a short-term or long-term basis. Homebound Bible study refers to a Sunday School teacher or member visiting and sharing Bible truths on a weekly or monthly basis.

The *Special Delivery* homebound ministry resources provide an administrative guide for those who wish to begin this program. *Special Delivery* resources include a teacher packet and member leaflets. Order them by calling 1-800-458-2772.

Churches may also choose to adapt ongoing dated Bible study resources for a homebound ministry. Volunteers use the passage, commentary, and appropriate learning activities provided. Homebound visitors can also deliver sermon tapes and magazines.

In addition to these ideas, consider having one or more teachers record his/her own lesson each Sunday for duplication and delivery to the homebound during the week. This ministry requires persons who drive and several portable tape players. A prepared tape of several lessons is listed on the quarterly literature order form from LifeWay Christian Resources. These lessons can be separated onto individual tapes with music and personal words added.

Conference Call Sunday School Class

This provides a Sunday School class for homebound members who want to be taught each Sunday morning during Sunday School.

A person who speaks clearly over the telephone can present the lesson in a brief and concise manner. Arrange with your local telephone company to set up the conference call class on Sundays at the time you specify. Determine who wants to be in the class and give their phone numbers to the telephone company.

The telephone company will call all of the people in the class and get them on the line, then call the church with everyone ready to participate. Allow class members to talk for a few minutes before the presentation. Deliver member books to participants each quarter so they can study the lesson.

Read-the-Bible-Through Emphasis

Encourage senior adults to lead the church in a project to read the Bible through during the calendar year. A natural time to begin this emphasis is January 1. Suggested daily passages are found in adult Sunday School quarterlies, *Open Windows* devotional magazine, and *Baptist Adults,* a periodical for ongoing discipleship in the church.

Bible Conferences

Like adult VBS, this is a special Bible study emphasis taught over five days. Your pastor or well-known Bible teacher could teach the study. Generally, you would offer the teacher an honorarium. Plan at least an hour and a half each day with special music and a short break with light refreshments. If you use a morning schedule, incorporate a luncheon each day—either a covered dish or a meal provided for a small fee.

Invite your community to attend. Consider using the Winter Bible Study materials produced by LifeWay Christian Resources. It includes member books and Expository Notes for the teacher. A resource kit provides overhead transparencies and masters for copying.

Chapter 4

Transformational Discipleship

by Ralph Hodge, John Franklin, and Betty Hassler

What Is Transformational Discipleship?
Discipling Senior Adults
Barriers That Hinder Transformation
Transformational Discipleship and a Balanced Ministry
Involving Younger Seniors in Discipleship
Designing a Transformational Discipleship Strategy

A disciple is a follower of Jesus. Early believers were called Christians because they were trying to imitate Christ (Acts 11:26). Today's believers should be evaluated by the same criteria: Can others identify us as those who have "been with Jesus" (Acts 4:13)?

Can a person who has "been with Jesus" ever be the same again? An encounter with Jesus should lead to a transformed life. Transformed lives should result in a transformed church, transformed communities, and world impact.

We believe a transformational approach to discipleship will enable your senior adult ministry to increase in numbers, quality, and ministry while impacting the community around them. We will suggest ways to address the needs of seniors and lead them to be more productive and obedient Christians.

What Is Transformational Discipleship?
Transformational discipleship is a process that helps believers become conformed to the image of Christ. The goal of transformational discipleship is measured in Christlike character and conduct.

51

Transformational discipleship stands in contrast to discipling methods that focus on gaining information about the Christian life or on performing acts of service and ministry. Although believers should look for opportunities to grow and serve, neither knowledge nor service is the test of discipleship. Obedience is that test.

Jesus criticized the Pharisees for practicing empty religion, although they were known for their much knowledge and pious actions. Transformational discipleship aims for deeper life change than knowledge or good deeds. It seeks to give meaning and substance to Bible information while enlivening and empowering acts of service. This approach helps believers develop a love relationship with God through Christ that calls for growth/service from that motive alone.

Transformational discipleship does not so much change the practice of discipleship as it changes the focus. Instead of focusing on scheduling courses and ministry actions, the focus is on producing transformed Christians. Churches will always need biblically-based studies and opportunities to minister. However, a new focus on "image-bearing" enables these efforts to produce disciples.

Jesus Modeled Transformational Discipleship

Jesus came to show us what God is like, to restore our relationship with God through His sacrificial death on the cross, and to model for believers a life that is pleasing to God. From the life of Jesus, we can discern three key characteristics of a disciple.
- a deepening relationship with God
- a deepening relationship with the body (the church)
- a deepening relationship with the world

The following questions lead us to reflect on our relationship with God (the vertical test):
- Are my thoughts, attitudes, and actions becoming more like Jesus?
- Do I eagerly seek opportunities to worship and praise God?

- Do I eagerly seek prayer and Bible study times?
- How do I handle difficult situations that require sacrifice?
- How do I deal with trials?

These questions lead us to reflect on our relationship with believers (the horizontal test):

- To what degree do I love my brothers and sisters in Christ?
- To what degree do I love those who are difficult to love?
- How do I respond to conflict with another believer?
- How quickly do I forgive?
- Am I bothered by immature Christians?

These questions lead us to reflect on our relationship to the world:

- To what degree do I love the lost?
- How am I influencing those around me?
- Do I invest my resources in expanding God's kingdom?

At first glance a deepening relationship with God and with believers may seem contradictory to a deepening relationship with the world. Don't Christians need to be separate from the world? Fortunately, Jesus modeled how we should live as Christians reflecting His image. We will manage the tension between the three characteristics of a disciple as we:

- relate to the Father as Jesus related to the Father
- relate to the body as Jesus related to the body
- relate to the world as Jesus related to the world.

Rather than retreating from the non-Christian world, we are to be faithful representatives of Christ, telling the world separated by sin that forgiveness and reconciliation is through Him (see 1 Cor. 5:9-11). Our daily lives are to be a witness to Jesus' redeeming love.

Jesus Discipled His Followers

Jesus met with his disciples individually to discern their spiritual progress (see John 21:15-23). He met with them by twos and threes (see John 1:35-39). He taught them as a small group (see Matt. 10).

He preached to multitudes with them by His side (see John 6:1-14). We can summarize Jesus' discipling principles in two words:

- **Accountable**—Jesus and His disciples had an accountability relationship. Jesus was transparent with His disciples; He was not so much concerned with teaching facts as He was intent on their knowing His heart, His passion, His character. With Peter He displayed great joy and great pain. He rejoiced when Peter called Him the Christ and agonized when Peter refused to let Him wash Peter's feet. Accountability involves willingness to confront an errant brother. It requires a heart for repentance; it gladly asks for and offers forgiveness.

- **Transferable**—The small group was not just a warm, fuzzy bonding experience but rather a launching pad for worldwide missions. The disciples grew closer to Jesus so that they could do the work Jesus had called them to do. Jesus' charge to Peter was, "Feed my sheep" (John 21:17). Jesus' discipling methods produced disciple-makers (see Luke 10).

Measuring Spiritual Growth (Transformation)

We usually evaluate discipleship programs in our churches by a head count—how many people are enrolled in courses—or by the number of courses offered. We know that knowledge does not necessarily equal change. We cannot assume that completing a course of study has had a transformational impact on a believer.

Neither can we assume that acts of service are motivated by a transformed heart. Can a church member serve on the board of a rescue mission and engage in dishonest business practices? Can a man faithfully witness to others yet mistreat his wife and children?

Programming will never automatically produce transformation. However, programming can be a tool God uses to effect transformation in a believer's life. The tool (a course of study) must never be confused with the product (a transformed life).

Realistically speaking, evaluating transformational discipleship requires much more time, patience, and prayer on the part of the leader. Leading a course or organizing a ministry is much easier than reading the condition of the human heart. How do we function as "fruit-inspectors" without becoming judgmental or self-righteous (see Matt. 7:16-20)?

Some suggest evaluation of spiritual growth is far too subjective to measure and thus unproductive. Certainly, we should approach efforts to evaluate it with caution. Attempts to measure Christlikeness by instruments such as checklists, rating scales, or continuums may lead to legalism and self-absorption. We become consumed with our own progress and take our eyes off Christ and the relationship.

The temptation to smug self-righteousness is well-illustrated by Jesus' account of the prayers of the Pharisee and tax collector (see Luke 18:9-14). The Pharisee used some of the right criteria with a totally wrong motive. He succeeded in proving himself righteous in his own eyes! Humility demonstrates an awareness of the righteousness of God and of Christ's righteousness through which we are redeemed.

However, we would not have been given the command to imitate Christ if there were no means of evaluating our progress. Jesus encouraged His disciples to look for evidence of transformation and to celebrate when it was demonstrated (see Luke 7:44-50).

The standard by which we measure transformational discipleship is a growing love relationship with the Father through Christ. This relationship with the Father produces growth in Christlikeness. The result is changed lives that impact the world.

When this criteria is kept before the church and referenced as a part of each discipleship experience, the focus of discipleship will be clear. This focus will give meaning and purpose to courses of study and acts of service.

Discipling Senior Adults

When she was in her 80s, a wonderful senior adult Christian Corrie Ten Boom, was asked by a child, "Are you old?" She replied with a twinkle in her eye, "No, I'm not old. Why, I'm young, but, sweetheart, I've been young for a long, long time."

Often, senior adults are treated as though they were a different kind of creature, unlike younger adults. Actually, they may be more similar to than different from other age groups in basic spiritual needs. Seniors are still dealing with many of the same temptations as younger adults. To categorize them as though they were not still in the ageless war of the flesh and the spirit does them a disservice.

In fact, the older one becomes, the greater the possibility that negative influences as well as positive ones have shaped his or her spiritual life. Years of life may cause a senior adult to grow further away from God as well as closer. A disappointing or hurtful experience in our relationship to the Lord many years ago can become a hardened pattern much more difficult to confront—and much easier to justify in our own minds—than when we were younger. Some circumstance or tragedy may become a major barrier to obedience as we make the changes in our roles and needs in later years. Temper, impatience, gossip, and a critical spirit are examples of traits that can infect all Christians at whatever age.

We recognize the temptations bombarding our youth and young adults. We often do not recognize that a whole new arsenal of temptations bombards senior adults. Adults living 20 to 30 years longer than their spouses face temptations and moral questions seldom faced by previous generations. Retirement with 25 or 30 years of relatively healthy life ahead brings new opportunities and new threats. Senior adults often face these challenges with less family support and understanding than afforded the life transitions and needs of younger people.

Senior adults need the church's help to grow in Christlikeness in their varied roles—leaders, parents, grandparents, spouses, employees, volunteers—and as they face changes and losses in the senior years. Discipleship includes helping seniors look to Christ for a healthy view of aging and appropriate responses to the changes they face.

Although meeting physical, social, and emotional needs of seniors is an important function of senior adult ministry, the ultimate goal of the discipling process is to glorify God. Our focus must always be on Him.

One of the most meaningful metaphors for personal spiritual transformation is the scene described in Jeremiah. God told Jeremiah to go down to the potter's house. There he saw the potter shaping clay into a vessel. Seeing that the clay was marred, the potter then shaped it into another vessel according to what he knew was the best use of this clay (see Jer. 18:1-4).

Like the potter, God applies pressure where needed and withholds pressure when best to transform us into the very likeness of Christ. Aging adults need to see God's hand in the pressures and events of life in the senior years. The church must not take for granted that older adults can interpret God's work in their lives.

Seniors may be new Christians or newly rededicated to growing in the Lord. We must not assume that everyone with gray hair grew up in church or knows the Bible from cover to cover. Some individuals really only begin to blossom for the Lord after the seasoning of many years.

Barriers That Hinder Transformation

Removing barriers to spiritual growth requires the power of the Holy Spirit. Satan custom designs some barriers for the specific personality and weaknesses of each of us. Other barriers are a generic one-size-fits all! Satan has to give little attention to creating these. We gladly erect them ourselves!

Busyness is a barrier for many seniors. Although we should encourage active lifestyles and continuing involvement in church and community, activities should never crowd out spiritual growth. An opposite barrier is boredom. Some seniors seem to find nothing new, interesting, or exciting about their spiritual journey. Bible study is ho-hum and Solomon's words ring true to them: "There is nothing new under the sun" (Eccl. 1:9).

Others are cynical about the likelihood of their developing Christlike character. Perhaps they have struggled with a besetting sin for many years, or they feel powerless in their prayer life.

Of all the barriers to discipleship, distraction probably requires the least effort from Satan. If being transformed into the likeness of Christ occurs through an intimate relationship with Him, then Satan surely works to distract us from all that a growing relationship requires. The longer a person lives, the greater the potential for losing a single-minded focus on our relationship with Christ.

A NASA scientist explained that deep inside spacecraft being propelled toward an orbit in space there is a computer program. It is designed to receive a signal signified by the Greek letter *delta*. The *delta* measures the difference between the course the rocket is supposed to take and the course it is actually on. Although a rocket may be off course more time than on course, there is no damage as long as the *delta* signal is measured and the computer corrects the course of the rocket from time to time.

A church's discipleship program provides a means for course correction. Discipleship that focuses on our relationship with Jesus will provide a spiritual *delta* to guide our spiritual journey.

Transformational Discipleship and a Balanced Ministry

In the previous chapter the author spoke of life-changing Bible study. How does a properly functioning Bible study program fit hand-in-glove with a transformational discipleship program. Are either expendable?

We believe both are necessary ingredients to a balanced spiritual life. The purpose of each program area of the church explains the difference in strategy. The Bible Teaching-Reaching organization (Sunday School) intentionally reaches out to the unsaved and unchurched. Bible Teaching-Reaching is the evangelism arm of the church. Discipleship groups, on the other hand, seek to strengthen believers, including those who are new in Christ.

Sunday School generally meets at a given time and place during the week. Discipleship occurs throughout the week—mornings, noontime, evenings, and weekends—both inside and outside the church. Sunday School has an on-going class roll. Discipleship groups meet for 1 month or 6 to 12 weeks. Once groups have met for a few sessions, they may be closed to new attendees.

In Sunday School the curriculum is the Bible itself. Discipleship groups study the Bible topically, meeting around spiritual growth issues of interest or concern. The Sunday School curriculum must be entry-level for non-Christians as well as mature Christians. Discipleship groups can use resources that provide in-depth study of particular aspects of the Christian life.

Without the Sunday School organization, churches grow inward not outward and may lose their focus on the Great Commission. Without discipleship, Sunday School members may grow numerically but not mature in Christlike character and conduct.

A balanced senior adult ministry utilizes the full component of programs and organizations within the church to grow disciples. Missions, worship, music, ministries, recreation and social events—all work together to produce transformation.

Evaluating Discipleship Experiences

As we apply the transformational model to the discipling experiences in our churches, two evaluation criteria should be used:

1. Do they produce accountability?

   Discipleship groups should lead spiritually growing senior adults to establish accountability relationships for spiritual growth, setting the example for all ages in the church.

"A Christian is not a loner, he is a member of the body of Christ....Be accountable to one another. Your corporate responsibility in the priesthood of believers is to help each other function as a part of a core of people who pray together, and in whom God moves mightily."[1]

Accountability requires a level of transparency uncommon in most church groups. It also calls for loving confrontation, repentance, and forgiveness. Effectiveness is judged by what kind of people we are becoming. A spiritually-minded person is growing in "joy, peace, patience, kindness, goodness, faithfulness, gentleness and self-control" (Gal. 5:22). Accountability groups call us to compare ourselves with Jesus and not each other (see 2 Cor. 10:12).

2. Are they transferable?

Discipleship groups should lead spiritually growing senior adults to transfer what they learn in small-group experiences to service and ministry in the church and in the world. The effectiveness or success of discipleship is reflected in Christians becoming more like Jesus in loving, witnessing, serving, and ministering to others. Instead of more classes or more activities, the goal is developing a heart for God and a heart for people.

Establish the objective that senior adult discipleship through your church is going to develop disciples who develop disciples. Jesus commanded us to be disciplers (see Matt. 28:19-20). Like witnessing, discipling is not a special gift but an anointed lifestyle. Whether by intention or as an overflow of our lives, we are all disciple-makers. The big question is whether we are good or bad disciple-makers.[2]

Helping senior adults grow in spiritual maturity includes helping them become more effective witnesses and disciple-makers, leading others to be transformed into the likeness of Jesus. Transferability keeps accountability groups from becoming ingrown.

Selecting Resources

Discipleship groups are usually formed around topical issues. When choosing resources for such groups, apply this test: Does the resource help a person develop a growing love relationship with the Father through the Son that leads to growth in Christlikeness?

Place these three statements over the content of the resources:

- Does the resource provide faithful biblical guidance for Christians to deepen their relationship with God? The resource should help us relate to the Father as Jesus related to the Father. It should help us to know Christ and grow in our relationship with Him more than ever before.
- Does the resource provide faithful biblical guidance for Christians to deepen their relationship with the body (church)? Are Christians drawn to a deeper love for the body of Christ and feel compelled to fulfill their God-given responsibility as a part of the body (see 1 Cor. 12:12-31)?
- Does the resource provide faithful biblical guidance for Christians to relate to the world as Jesus related to the world? Will persons completing the study have help in determining actions and decisions in a world that turns from Christ? Will completing the study provide help to live in the world but not of the world (see John 17:14-18)?

Grouping Seniors for Discipleship

Small groups remain the best avenue for helping Christians assess their personal, spiritual journeys. This person-to-person, relational setting allows Christians to honestly reveal spiritual needs and accept correction from those who know and love them.

Individuals can be involved in discipleship through a variety of small-group experiences.

- Ongoing group. The same core group of persons meets together indefinitely. They study a variety of subjects and resources. The group chooses the day, time, and place.

- Short-term study. A topic (course) is announced. People belong to the group only while the study is being conducted. A group remains together only if they choose to study another topic together. Day, time, and place vary with each group. The leader leads for the duration of the study.
- Support group. Formed to help persons heal from personal or emotional issues, groups meet for 6-12 weeks or longer in a confidential and supportive setting. Some groups close to new members after two to three sessions while others remain open throughout.
- Individual study. Used by persons who cannot participate in group study due to travel or other restrictions.
- One-to-one study. A more mature or experienced person (encourager or mentor) helps another learn in a semi-private setting.
- Men's or women's groups who study topics dealing with gender-based issues.
- Couple-to-couple friendship or mentoring relationships where a discipleship experience is built into fellowship/recreational activities.
- Retreat setting. A topical study is discussed at a weekend or three-day retreat. Participants complete the study on their own prior to the retreat. The retreat provides an opportunity to process the information and make applications.

Small groups are usually based on similarities between members. Called affinity groups, they major on lifestyle issues and seek to attract persons with particular needs. Affinity groupings may reflect one's marital status—single persons, divorced, widowed, or re-married. They may be based on gender or work status (employed, retired) or on location (snowbirds, campers).

When forming affinity groups, consider common needs such as caring for spouses or parents with illnesses such as Alzheimer's. Caregiver support groups encourage senior adults who provide care for their parents or elderly relatives, either in their own homes or elsewhere. Grief support groups bring together persons who need to process their grief experience. Some seniors are grandparents and thus prospects for a grandparenting course. Other seniors are parents of teenagers and would like to process their experiences with other parents of teens.

Affinity groups can be scheduled any time of the day, any day of the week. Daytime discipleship groups cater to persons who do not drive after dark. The most frequent reason seniors give for not attending evening meetings has to do with vision. A second concern is safety and security. Encourage your seniors to identify the best time, place, and day of the week for discipleship groups to meet.[3]

Involving Younger Seniors in Discipleship

Baby boomers began turning 50 in 1996. This generation has not traditionally supported church programs with the loyalty characteristic of the two generations before them.

In churches where discipleship continues to be offered primarily on Sunday evenings, boomers may respond negatively. They may choose to spend that time with their families, go on an outing, or prepare for the workweek.

Instead of presenting discipleship as a program, treat it as a way of life. Study opportunities are means to a larger goal of becoming Christlike in character and conduct. Make study opportunities convenient for younger seniors who travel, those who continue to work, those who are caregivers for the frail elderly, and so forth. Offer individualized study, mentors, groups that meet at times other than Sunday evenings, weekend retreats, and morning or evening short-term groups.

Younger seniors look for a return on their investment. They will be critical of courses that do not meet their standards of quality. Study materials must pass the meaningfulness test: How will this help me be a more productive and obedient Christian in the world?

Younger seniors are also doers, more than hearers. Courses on subjects such as leadership and personal development, witnessing, ministry evangelism, and prayer which lead to specific actions such as community ministries, workplace prayer groups, or missions involvement will be preferred over those that focus on knowing content.

In summary, here are some characteristics of a discipling process that will appeal to younger seniors:

1. Choices in time, day, length, and method of study.
2. Short-term studies rather than long-term studies.
3. Quality resources and leaders.
4. Topics of personal interest and immediate application.
5. Studies that lead to meaningful impact on the world.

Designing a Transformational Discipleship Strategy

Communicating a renewed focus on discipleship as a transformational process will require thoughtful preparation. What process can we put into place that will lead seniors to embrace discipleship as a lifestyle as opposed to an activity on the church calendar? What will encourage those who are not presently involved in a discipleship group to rethink this need in their lives?

Fertilize the Soil.

Pray! Ultimately, only God changes people. Prayer excuses neither poor planning nor laziness, but many can testify to superb organization and hard work with no results. Pray for God's power and wisdom in building a discipleship ministry. His leading largely determines the success of your ministry.

Begin Talking About What You Are Hearing from God.

Tell others formally and informally what you are sensing about God's leading. The Holy Spirit will confirm His direction in others as you bear witness to God's direction in your life.

Watch for God's Timing.

How do you discern God's timing? Listen to what senior adults are saying. When they begin to express a need to grow, it is God's time. What if there is no response? If you try to proceed before God has had time to work the desire for discipleship in their hearts, then your efforts will fail. Be patient and trust that God is working to accomplish His goals in His people. Meanwhile, keep praying and keep bearing witness to the need for lifestyle discipleship.

Watch to See Whose Heart God Is Touching.

God calls those He wants. Usually, He builds the need first in those He wants to use as leaders.

Pull Together Leaders Who Have a Heart for Discipleship.

In the Bible, when leaders were sensitive to God's direction, the impact was long-lasting and far-reaching. When the leaders were not growing disciples themselves, they tried to squelch God's activity and hindered the work. Be patient and spend the extra time necessary with your leaders until God grows in them a heart for discipleship. Then they will be your strongest allies.

Enlist leaders of senior adult discipleship groups who have a heart for discipleship. Don't be age-biased when talking with potential leaders. One effective discipleship group of senior adults is lead by a 48-year-old man who was mentored by the previous leader of the group. It was a natural process for the younger man to assume leadership. The group believed God had been preparing him for this time.

Lynn Anderson points out that the shepherd is a major metaphor for leadership in the Bible. Shepherds carried sheep when they were injured, held them to feed them when they were weak, and literally lived with the sheep. Shepherds were easily identified when they came into the village marketplace after months in the fields caring for sheep. They smelled like sheep! Anderson encourages us to identify potential leaders by their lifestyles. They are seen caring for and ministering to people.[4]

Retreat With a Planning Group to Seek God's Plan for Your Church.

Church leaders are finding members less and less responsive to ministries that they have not had a direct part in conceiving, conceptualizing, and planning. As you think about enhancing or beginning senior adult discipleship in your church, involve seniors in the decision-making process. They will be the chief proponents of what they have helped plan.

Determine God's Desired Outcomes. Set Goals.

Ask God, What are You trying to do in the lives of senior adults that the discipleship ministry can help accomplish? God knows your senior adults and what they can accomplish for His kingdom. Ask for and receive His wisdom.

Then set goals. Goals may include numbers of persons and activities, but as you set goals recall the purpose of discipling. Use subjective criteria that emphasizes growth in Christlikeness.

Look at Senior Adult Needs.

Ask senior adults in your church and community, How can the church meaningfully impact your life? Talk to senior adults who are not active in any church. Question doctors and nurses, social workers, and people in businesses that depend on knowing the needs of senior adults.

Listen to uncover needs below the surface level. For instance, I (Ralph) was involved in a listening session with 30 senior adults in a local church. When asked how their church could help them, they came up with several issues. These seniors needed help in knowing how to fulfill God's purposes for them as older parents of children who now have children. Not only did they need to know how to be godly grandparents, but also how to be godly parents to their grown children.

The listening session identified a second major issue of concern—the declining evidence of character and biblical morality in the actions and lives of senior adults. As a result, groups were begun that focused on ethical issues in the workplace and in relationships.

Work with senior adults to develop a program that fits the senior adults you are committed to serve. Take seriously the wisdom of Scripture: "By wisdom a house is built, and through understanding it is established; through knowledge its rooms are filled with rare and beautiful treasures" (Prov. 24:3-4).

Ask, What Resources Are Available to Meet Needs?

Resources include leadership, facilities, financial support, and published materials. For a catalog of current discipleship materials that combine the best of biblical scholarship and small-group methodology, write Discipleship and Family Adult Department, MSN 151, 127 Ninth Avenue N., Nashville, TN 37234 or visit your nearest Baptist Book Store or LifeWay Christian Store.

Provide the Organization and Leadership

The best planning incorporates both long-term and short-term objectives. Planning should always be viewed as an organism, allowed to change and develop with the real needs of real people and the leadership of God.

Short-term planning allows you to be responsive to current issues within the current membership. Long-term planning recognizes that there are prescriptives for discipleship that have been true for the people of God down through the ages. Every disciple needs to grow in prayer and worship, for example.

A minimal organization includes a discipleship training director elected by the church and small-group leaders selected for the duration of a course of study. The coordinating leader of senior adult ministries and the person charged with directing the church discipleship program should work together to maintain accountability and communication with the church, provide administrative support for each discipleship group, and facilitate the training and support of group leaders.

Some senior adult ministries may choose to select a senior adult discipleship director who works with the church discipleship director to form small groups and secure resource materials.

For detailed information on beginning a discipleship ministry in your church, call for the booklet, "Leading Discipleship in a Church," 1-800-458-2772, or ask for item 0-7673-2961-9 at your nearest Baptist Book Store or Lifeway Christian Store.

Trained consultants from LifeWay Christian Resources are available to answer your questions or offer suggestions. Call 1-800-251-2824. You may also talk to your local Baptist association director of discipleship or to someone in the discipleship department of your state Baptist convention.

Implement the Plan.
Put the plan to work. Keep the focus on producing disciples, not counting heads.

Evaluate the Plan
Develop a system to evaluate discipleship using the criteria mentioned under the heading "Measuring Spiritual Growth," pages 54-55. Criteria must include:

> **Accountability**—Are discipling groups holding each other accountable for developing a deepening relationship with God, other believers, and the lost world.

> **Transferability**—Are discipling groups producing disciples who produce disciples?

The effectiveness or success of discipleship is reflected in Christians becoming more like Jesus in witnessing, serving, ministering, and loving. Once this focus is established, continue to apply the criteria Jesus used in evaluating His own ministry:

- relate to the Father as Jesus related to the Father
- relate to the body as Jesus related to the body
- relate to the world as Jesus related to the world.

Jesus said, "Now this is eternal life: that they may know you, the only true God, and Jesus Christ, whom you have sent" (John 17:3). Everything we do should lead us to growth in an intimate personal love relationship with the Father and Son. The *relationship* produces the Christlikeness!

---

[1]Henry Blackaby, "Revival Notes," *Experiencing God Report,* n.d., 3.

[2]John Phillips, *Only One Life* (Neptune, NJ: Loizeaux Brothers, Inc., 1995), 89. Used by permission of Loizeaux Brothers, Inc., Neptune, New Jersey.

[3]Roy Edgemon and Steve Williams, *Leading Discipleship in a Church* (Nashville: Convention Press, 1997), 41, 47.

[4]Anderson, Lynn, *They Smell Like Sheep* (West Monroe, LA: Howard Publishing Co., 1997).

Chapter 5

Caring Ministries

by Robert Sheffield and David Apple

Discover Ministry Needs of Senior Adults
Involve the Caring Team in Meeting Needs
Care for Three Distinct Age Groups
Observe Key Principles for Ministering to Seniors
Practice Active Loving
Minister to Senior Adults Through Sunday School
Provide Caring Ministries

One of the greatest challenges facing the church involves ministering to the ever-increasing number of older adults in our congregations. How can we care for seniors who need assistance while at the same time utilizing able seniors in ministry to each other, the larger congregation, and the community?

Caring ministries of the church are professionally referred to as pastoral ministries. Pastoral ministry in the broadest sense refers to the activity of any Christian who seeks to meet the specific needs of another person in the name of Christ. Based on the servant model of Jesus, pastoral ministers stand alongside fellow believers as they go through the crises of living and connect them with the resources of the church and community. Deacons, Sunday School leaders, and members are pastoral ministers as they offer care and concern to others. In its narrower sense, pastoral ministry refers to the activity of professional clergy or church staff ministers who care for the needs of individuals in the church or community. In this chapter we will refer to pastoral ministries as caring ministries.

Whether you are in a church where seniors comprise the majority of your congregation or seniors are in the minority, this chapter will help you identify pastoral ministry needs and strategically plan for what you can do in your unique church situation.

Discover Ministry Needs of Senior Adults

Although the aging process has unique aspects, most seniors face problems all of us deal with at one time or another. These problems include health, employment, finances, loneliness, losses, and need for recognition, purpose, and meaning. For seniors these needs are concentrated in a few years and often are in crisis proportions.

We can identify some of these needs by looking at Isaiah 61:1-3. Jesus referred to this passage as the focus for His ministry in Luke 4:18-19. As you read the passage below, underline the kinds of people Jesus targeted for ministry. In the margin, list ways your church seeks to address the needs of these individuals.

> The Spirit of the Sovereign Lord is on me, because the Lord has anointed me to preach good news to the poor. He has sent me to bind up the brokenhearted, to proclaim freedom for the captives and release from darkness for the prisoners, to proclaim the year of the Lord's favor and the day of vengeance of our God, to comfort all who mourn, and provide for those who grieve in Zion—to bestow on them a crown of beauty instead of ashes, the oil of gladness instead of mourning, and a garment of praise instead of a spirit of despair (Isa. 61:1-3).

In this passage Jesus points us to people who are:

Poor—Adequate financial resources is a critical issue for seniors. A woman asked a friend how retirement was going. She replied, "I have twice as much husband and half as much money." In this age of two-income families, retirees living on fixed incomes may find

71

themselves near or at the poverty level. The worry of an unexpected major expense or health problem robs their peace of mind. The threat of poverty can be as stressful as poverty itself.

In addition to financial limitations, many older adults experience poverty in regard to relationships. Long-term friends have moved away or died. They may not know where or how to find new friends. Other seniors face a poverty of self-image. Our society devalues the wisdom of age. Seniors want to be viewed as individuals with worthwhile contributions to make to their families, friends, and community. Instead, they may perceive themselves as lacking financial resources, friends, and self-esteem.

Captives–Most persons would automatically associate "imprisoned" with "incarceration." Older adults, however, may feel imprisoned by poor health, alcohol or prescription drug dependency, lack of transportation or physical mobility, abuse, guilt, materialism, or habitual sins. Those who live as "prisoners"–unable to break the chains of their own or other's making–need release from the sense of isolation and shame they feel.

Mourning–Seniors experience the loss of loved ones, especially as they reach the middle to late senior years. Intense loneliness heads the list of grief issues. In addition to loss of loved ones, many seniors grieve the loss of employment or productivity, physical capabilities, ability to care for themselves, or other disappointments and setbacks.

Brokenhearted or in despair–Hopelessness plagues many older adults. Some fear or have experienced loss of control over major decisions facing them. Many worry about or are disappointed by family members, finances, failures, and the future. Others have lost a sense of personal identity. They need to develop a new vision for their lives during retirement. Depression in people aged 65 years and older is a major public health problem. White men older than 80 are six times more likely to commit suicide than any other demographic group in the United States.[1]

Although the picture painted in Isaiah 61 may appear bleak, Jesus came so that crowns of beauty might replace ashes. In our efforts to care for the majority of seniors who are active and healthy, we must not overlook those who need specialized ministry.

Involve the Caring Team in Meeting Needs

Many of the needs we have identified—poor self-esteem, isolation, mourning, hopelessness—represent emotional issues with spiritual overtones. The caring team of the church is uniquely equipped to offer emotional and spiritual care. Your caring team includes the ministry of the pastor, staff members, and deacons. Your caring team also includes Sunday School leadership, as caregiving is a stated purpose of a well-functioning Bible study class and department. Let's begin by looking at the role of the pastor, staff, and deacons. Later in the chapter, we will consider the role of the Sunday School.

Role of the pastor—The pastor serves as the leader for the caring ministries of the church. In fact, the pastor must lead the way in actively seeking ways to care for and involve seniors in ministry. Instead of looking at seniors as a liability, the pastor must consider them a valuable resource. He must see them as a key component in the life of the church body.

During a conference on church growth, a young pastor asked the conference leader how he could reach more senior adults. The surprised conference leader did not hear this request very often. He inquired, "Why do you ask?"

The pastor replied, "My church is reaching so many young people and young adults that we need the influence and wisdom of some older adults." This attitude needs to typify pastors in their approach to ministry with seniors. Pastors who value seniors will convey that attitude to the congregation.

With the weight of responsibility most pastors carry, the tasks of developing ministries to and for seniors must be shared with a team. Often, another staff member will be designated as coordinator of senior adult ministries. In some cases, a layperson is selected. The coordinator works with all aspects of senior adult work to ensure that needs are met and services are rendered.

Ideally, the coordinator will work with a steering committee made up of leaders of the various senior adult programs and activities. (See p. 26 for an organizational model for a balanced senior adult ministry.) When the pastor works through a coordinator and steering committee, he is employing the biblical image of the shepherd utilizing the "lead sheep" to guide the flock into safe and nourishing pastures.

Pastors need to lead out in seeing that the needs of seniors are met. Pastors should not be expected to carry the entire weight of visiting the homebound, hospitalized, bereaved, despondent or lonely seniors in their congregations. By delegating tasks and supervising other key leaders, pastors can effectively shepherd the flock by modeling servant leadership and encouraging and affirming those who are called to service with and for seniors.

Role of church staff—In many churches the pastor serves as the only staff member. In larger congregations with additional staff, he may designate another staff person to coordinate ministries for older adults. Whichever situation describes your church, the pastor still serves as the key leader for pastoral care.

The minister of music is often delegated as coordinator of senior adult ministries because of his active participation with a senior adult choir. The choir may be the group that takes trips, plans retreats, sponsors socials, and offers care to the church's senior adults. In other churches, the minister of education takes the lead in planning and coordinating senior adult activities, working primarily through the Sunday School organization. Still other churches designate the minister of recreation as coordinator because of his key role in programming through-the-week activities.

Churches are beginning to employ ministers to senior adults. Future projections indicate that ministers to senior adults will outnumber ministers to youth after the majority of baby boomers have entered the senior years.

Staff members who serve as senior adult coordinators should work through existing church programs and with a steering committee to ensure that seniors' needs are effectively met.

Role of deacons—Deacons play an important role in ministering to seniors. If the deacons in your church minister through the Deacon Family Ministry Plan, serving the needs of seniors is a natural outgrowth. In this plan, seniors are a part of a deacon's family group. Seniors may constitute a family living in their own home, they may live as a part of the family of one of their adult children, they may live in multi-unit housing, an assisted living facility, or nursing home.

As a part of a deacon's "family," seniors receive ministry. As deacons get to know their families, they get to know their needs. Deacons provide caring nurture, practical support, and spiritual reinforcement to the seniors in their family groupings.

Some churches organize their deacon ministries around the deacon team concept. Deacons choose or are assigned to teams that minister in a variety of ways, such as hospital visitation, prospect visitation, or benevolence ministries. In such a church, one deacon team might focus on ministering to seniors.

Deacons on a senior adult team should tailor their ministries to the needs in their church setting. Deacon ministry teams may offer a variety of services, depending on the skills and available time of its members. One church with whom I (Robert) worked had deacons who specialized in providing maintenance and repairs for the homes of senior adult members. Whether married or widowed, seniors were eligible to receive this help. This deacon ministry gave these seniors a feeling of being loved by their church family. They, in turn, held the deacons in high esteem.

Deacon teams allow deacons to minister in both the good times and the bad. Seniors do not have to wait for sickness or crises to arise before benefiting from deacon ministry. Their care is ongoing, with regular contact between the deacon team and senior adults.

Other churches have deacon ministry teams headed by a deacon but open to other members of the congregation who feel led or gifted in a certain area of ministry. A deacon-led senior adult ministry team composed of church volunteers can expand its ministry to include more extensive offerings. A list of services that can be provided for seniors is found at the end of this chapter.

Care for Three Distinct Age Groups

In order to avoid placing all senior adults in one uniform mold, think of them as three distinct age groups with specific caring ministry concerns.

1. **Younger seniors**—The major themes of pastoral care with "young" seniors are *enablement* and *challenge.* Enablement refers to the efforts of caring ministers to open doors for their continued participation in both church and community. Challenge refers to the efforts to help people grow and develop. These individuals need to finish the preparations for retirement and enter it with grace and hope.

   Some senior adults manage their retirement as a process rather than an event. They work out a gradual reduction in demands at a pace which fits their comfort zones. This plan gives them more leisure plus the satisfaction of work they enjoy.

   Other seniors who work one day and retire the next experience "retirement shock." The church can help individuals plan ahead. Seminars, retreats, and individual counseling can help seniors make a smooth transition.

   Younger seniors can also be challenged to mentor other adults in the congregation and to teach job and life skills through seminars and workshops. Many of them are in the stage of life when short-term mission involvement is possible. (Refer to pp. 115-125 for missions opportunities.)

76

2. **Middle seniors**—The key word to describe "middle" seniors is *contributing* because they continue to care greatly about the well-being of their communities, their families, and the church. Generally, members of this group are caregivers for others—either elderly parents or relatives, children or grandchildren, and peers. They contribute to the ministries of the church through giving, leadership, and participation. Do not neglect the input of this group. Cultivate their contributions by valuing their insights. They have a great desire and even a passion to see the church function as the Lord would have it.

    Middle seniors can be enlisted as key workers in ongoing ministries such as food pantries, clothing rooms, and transportation. They can be mobilized as church visitors and soul-winners. Because of their histories with the congregation, they can offer new member orientation, staff prayer rooms, volunteer in the church office, and serve on committees and task forces.

3. **Older seniors**—Only about 20 percent of seniors 65 or older report having to limit their activities because of impaired health. The other 80 percent continue to function in their own homes, in a retirement facility or with extended family. This group needs ministry in at least three ways:
    * coping with the crises that seem to happen more frequently
    * mobilizing a support system for continuing independence
    * continuity in times of change

    The central themes in caring with older seniors are *respect* and *closeness*. Respect refers to helping seniors retain personal dignity and independence. Demonstrate a reverence for age—a concept taught throughout the Bible. Show respect as you affirm a person's right to privacy and decision-making. Closeness indicates willingness to spend time with older seniors, especially those limited in their communication with the outside world. Do not "put them on a shelf." Plan ways intersect their lives.

Observe Key Principles for Ministering to Seniors

Pastors, staff members, deacons, Sunday School leaders, and lay volunteers minister more effectively as they observe basic principles for ministering to the needs of seniors. In *Equipping Deacons in Caring Skills,* Dr. Jerry Day, a Christian psychologist and counselor, points out the following principles:

Come to grips with your own aging. You cannot help seniors if you are not in touch with your own aging issues. You, too, will have similar needs one day.

Care "with" and not "for" seniors. Seniors need to feel they have as much independence as possible for as long as possible. Involve seniors in the activities you do on their behalf. Help them feel they contribute to their own well-being.

Instead of making decisions for them, give them the facts and related information they need to make good decisions. Far too often seniors feel like the person who said, "Now that I am at the point where I know the answers, nobody is asking me the questions." Respect seniors' choices, even if they are not choices you would make. Avoid a paternal attitude that reduces them to a childlike state.

Show respect for seniors. Our society has been youth-oriented for many years. Looking young has been valued while looking old has been denigrated. Seniors in your church need to feel the church is one place where gray hairs are valued (see Prov. 16:31).

Show respect by asking their opinions and listening attentively when they share their views on subjects of their own choosing. You do not have to agree with their views but value them enough to listen. In addition, respect the spiritual maturity of seniors. When we allow them to share their faith with us, they challenge us to grow in trust. Share these stories—with permission—with the church family.

Stand ready to mobilize any and all available resources at your disposal. Refer to the list of available resources within your community and church compiled by your senior adult steering committee (see p. 210). Use these resources as you minister.

Do not assume that occasional memory lapses indicate the presence of senility or other types of dementia. Experts tell us a definite difference exists between those with Alzheimer's and those who periodically cannot remember things. In the first case, the people can't remember but don't know they can't remember. In the second instance, individuals can't remember but have an awareness that they can't remember.

While memory loss may occur as individuals grow older, it does not necessarily indicate the presence of disease. Don't assume that senility has set in. Treat each situation as unique instead of stereotyping. Then you are better able to deal with each person as an individual with specific needs.

Minister to the extended family of senior adults. Many senior adults have family members nearby who deliver care and probably have done so for a long time. Some of the richest ministering times come when we have the opportunity to touch these individuals with a loving word or deed.[2]

Practice Active Loving

As you provide care for your senior adults, practice what Barbara Deane calls active loving. These skills can be easily learned. They include active listening, nonverbal touching, and giving positive reinforcement.[3]

Active Listening

In active listening, seek to get in touch with what the speaker feels and not what you feel about the situation. This practice contrasts empathetic listening–"I hear how you feel"–with sympathetic listening–"I feel just like you feel." Practice empathetic listening by restating the feelings that you heard.

Active listening helps us avoid simply reacting to what is said. The following dialogue serves as an example of active listening.

> *Senior:* I'm all alone. Nobody cares about me.
> *Normal response:* I care.
> *Active listening response:* It sounds to me like you're feeling
> isolated from people.[4]

Active listening requires us to stop talking, calm our minds, and focus on the person talking. We must resist the temptation to anticipate what the person will say next. Instead, listen intently to the words said and the feelings that lie behind the words. Very often you will hear what the person doesn't say as well as what she says. Barbara Deane shares what not to do in active listening.

- Don't correct.
- Don't attempt to argue the person out of his or her feelings.
- Don't judge.
- Don't feel you have to solve the problem.
- Don't give advice.
- Don't try to cheer the person up prematurely. It cuts off the full expression of feelings.
- Don't say, "I know just how you feel."[5]

Two additional don'ts: Don't listen to tell your own story. This response is called autobiographical listening. When you share your story at the first available opportunity in the conversation, the senior adult may withdraw and not feel heard. Sharing your story—when it is applicable—can come at a later time.

A second action to avoid is this: Don't divulge confidences. Since you will not always know what is privileged information, avoid repeating the conversation. When you need to relate information to another person on the caring team, be sure to ask permission. Avoid any hint of gossip.

Nonverbal touching

Another way to provide meaningful care involves nonverbal touching. Touch transmits care more powerfully than we can imagine.

The skin is the body's largest sense organ with millions of nerve endings. Without stimulation of the skin, human beings often experience an ache or longing that the medical world labels skin hunger. Whether or not you are touched can make a measurable physical difference to your body. Unfortunately, often nobody touches the elderly at a time when they've suffered many losses and need touching the most.[6]

The following paragraph contains some of the ways you can provide the touch seniors need. Before you read the paragraph, keep in mind that not all seniors respond to every one of these equally well. Each person has his or her "space" that should not be violated. Before you presume you can touch the person in a way that feels comfortable to you, ask permission and watch for the reaction.

You may give an appropriate hug, pat the shoulder, gently squeeze the arm, take the person's hand in yours and place it gently between your two hands, or offer your arm as support when you walk together. "If you can't do any of these, don't feel you must. You can encourage other family members" to provide this kind of care for the senior.[7]

Give positive reinforcement

Another helpful response focuses on giving positive reinforcement. Compliments sincerely given are like water to a thirsty plant. Take every opportunity to affirm seniors for major and minor accomplishments. When people feel better about themselves, feelings of worthlessness and despair often dissipate. Encourage seniors to be involved in worthwhile endeavors to the limit of their abilities.

Minister to Senior Adults Through Sunday School

Your church already has a group of dedicated, equipped people ready to serve as ministers to senior adults. Most churches call this group Sunday School teachers, care group leaders, and members. Utilize your Sunday School organization to multiply the number of persons involved in pastoral ministry.

Why include the Sunday School in the pastoral ministries of your church? Consider the following:

- The Sunday School is assigned the task of equipping and involving people in ministry. Ministry serves as a natural response to the needs of Sunday School members.
- Ministry furnishes a natural bridge to help persons recognize and respond to the redemptive work of Jesus. Applying the Bible to life is the primary focus of Bible teaching.
- The Sunday School's design permits it to target every person who is a church member or prospect.
- The organization of each class is designed to minister to members as well as nonmembers through care group or ministry teams.

Senior Adult Sunday School classes are among the best organized in most churches. Generally, they are motivated and able to meet the needs of members and prospects. However, depending on their ages and lifestyles, senior adult classes may be composed of persons who are themselves limited in their ability to help others. Perhaps they do not drive, or live on fixed incomes, or have health problems. The entire Sunday School organization can be mobilized to meet many of the needs identified by its older members.

First, let's consider how senior adult Sunday School classes can meet the needs of its own members and prospects. Then we will learn how the entire Sunday School organization can become involved.

Ministry Through Senior Adult Classes

Consider the following real-life situations. What could a class of senior adults do to provide ministry in each situation?

- George, age 71, has just been diagnosed with the same disease that claimed the lives of his three brothers.

- Audrey, a widow in her early sixties, lives next door to her 93-year-old mother. She would like to go out with her friends on occasion, but she does not feel she can leave her mother alone for more than an hour at a time.
- Gerald and Kathleen recently celebrated 55 years of marriage. His health confines him to their home most of the time. They do not go out socially nor have they attended church in several years.
- Buelah provides the primary care for her 50-year-old mentally retarded son. Within the last two years she lost her husband and her only other child. A Catholic, Buelah has expressed interest in attending her neighbor's Sunday School class but wonders what provision she would make for her son.
- At age 85, Betty still loves to travel. Her only relative lives across the country. Because of the expense, she must stay for an extended period of time when she visits. She misses her Sunday School class for months at a time.
- Margaret served as a Sunday School teacher for decades. Soon after her husband of 60 years died, she had a stroke. She had to move near her only relative and live in a nursing home. She feels very lonely.

In the paragraphs that follow, identify an organizational structure and specific actions a class could take to minister in each of the above situations.

1. **Care Groups**—Divide each senior adult Sunday School class into care groups of no more than five persons. Form the groups according to age, gender, geographical location of residences, marital status, or lifestyle. As the class grows in enrollment, form additional care groups so that everyone in the class benefits from assignment to a group.

    Within the care groups, assign one member as the care leader with the responsibility of contacting, ministering to, cultivating, and discipling as many as five assigned class members and prospects. Rotate care leaders on a yearly basis. Encourage them to involve other group members in discovering and meeting needs by accompanying them on ministry visits. Mentoring future care leaders can multiply the ministering arm of your Sunday School.

Care leaders visit or contact every member on a regular basis so they can keep informed of needs whether expressed or observed. Special ministry during the life transitions of members include but are not limited to retirement, illness, birth of a grandchild/great-grandchild, marriage, and bereavement. Other avenues for ministry include keeping in touch on special days such as birthdays, anniversaries, and special recognitions. Seniors particularly appreciate remembrances at these times.

Care leaders inform the teacher so that he or she can follow up with personal contact.

2. **Ministry Teams**—Sunday School classes have opportunities for long-term and short-term ministry projects. Some classes choose to organize ministry teams to implement these projects. Ministry teams may or may not consist of the same persons in a care group. Where both exist in a class, ministry teams assist with needs identified by the care groups. Ministry teams can take the place of care groups. In this case, each member of the ministry team receives contact and care by the team leader, in addition to having a specific ministry project assignment.

Usually, class members can choose which ministry team they want to join. Each team needs a leader who serves until the project is completed. The project may be ongoing, completed in a matter of months, or for a specific time period.

Classes should be organized for ministry action when an illness, death, natural calamity, financial need, or other emergency occurs among its members. On these occasions, timeliness is critical. A ministry team needs to be in place and ready to function. Some of these include visiting, listening to and/or counseling; providing food or flowers, sending cards and letters; setting up or donating to a memorial fund; collecting clothes and other items; providing care and/or house-sitting during a hospitalization or funeral; and assisting with cleaning, shopping, or transportation. The Adult Class Leader Administration Kit, available from LifeWay Christian Resources, provides suggestions for organizing the class for ministry.

In crisis situations, the Sunday School cooperates with other groups in the church to provide a comprehensive ministry approach. For example, many classes have a benevolence fund. Rarely will this fund have enough money to help in an extensive way. Working with the church staff, deacons, and/or the church benevolence ministry, the Sunday School class can deliver greater help.

Younger Adults Ministering to Senior Adults

In a church I (David) served, I enjoyed seeing a younger adult agree to be the department director for the oldest adult department. The seniors loved her and the feeling was mutual.

Ongoing ministry strategy to older adults requires a planned and coordinated effort. Services for senior adults should be coordinated by the person designated by the pastor as senior adult coordinator in cooperation with a senior adult steering committee. Usually, the Sunday School director and/or the director of the senior adult department(s) is on this committee. When various groups are brought together and their work is coordinated, ministry is more effective and more extensive than when any one group attempts to work alone.

Involve members in discovering and reporting needs. Some churches match a younger Sunday School department with an older department. Other churches match individuals or classes. Seniors prefer the same people to contact them. Too many different people can confuse older adults, who prefer those who know their history and preferences. Continuous contact creates a strong bond.

As members of younger Sunday School classes have contact with older church members, neighbors, friends, or relatives, they need a system for reporting the needs they uncover. Some churches use ministry report forms or prayer request cards for this purpose while others report these through newsletters and/or printed bulletins. Inform classes of how your church prefers to get the information.

However you report needs, have a plan in mind for follow up. Who receives the reports? How will class leaders know of these needs so they can lead class members to initiate action? When should the church staff and deacons become involved? How will the individual reporting know the need has been met?

Identify appropriate short-term and long-term actions to take. Once needs are discovered, plan ministry actions. Take advantage of the gifts and abilities of class members. They are more willing to perform ministry actions when they feel competent to help.

Provide Caring Ministries

The following list of caring ministries should stimulate your thinking about ways to meet your seniors' unique needs. (A church member survey similar to the one at the end of chap. 11, pp. 217-219, will help you identify persons interested in providing services.)

Grief Ministries

Seniors need a listening ear and a caring touch to help them through times of grief. Ministry by the pastor is especially important during this time. However, a busy pastor can only spend so much time with one grieving individual. The wise pastor will involve deacons and other trained laypersons in a grief ministry.

A deacon and spouse functioning as a ministering couple can provide an especially strategic grief ministry. If your deacon group has a functioning Deacon Family Ministry Plan, an avenue for grief ministry is already in place. However, grief ministry will require more time than other contacts with families. An additional grief ministry team, widows/widower support group, or one-on-one mentor to lead a person through the grief process can supplement the efforts of the pastor and deacons.

Letters and notes can also provide a meaningful way to keep in touch with seniors who experience grief. Homer Carter says, "Notes that affirm and express concern deepen and strengthen the relationship between deacons and others. When he [Deacon Russ] is away from the city on his many business trips, he writes notes and gives special attention to those he knows suffer from loneliness. However, he writes: 'I don't believe in using the telephone or letter writing as a substitute for personal contacts.'"[8]

Caregiver Support Groups

In many instances, family members provide the primary caregiving for senior adults. Seventy percent of caregivers nationwide are themselves senior adults. One senior adult couple had both fathers in their home at the same time. Support groups link those in the church who share the ongoing responsibility of caregiving.

Substitute Caregivers

Substitute caregivers stay with a homebound person for a few hours each week or over a weekend to allow the relative or caregiver a break from responsibility. No special training is required.

Employment Services

Some seniors may find themselves in need of help in finding part-time employment. Church members can share information about available jobs, offer job counseling, help seniors fill out applications, or prepare resumes. Classes or mentoring to update computer skills and other job skills supplement this service.

Visiting Friends
Visiting Friends are volunteers who commit to visiting a nursing home patient at least once a week. Begin with members of your church. As the ministry grows, discover patients with few visitors or little family support. Assign a volunteer to each patient.

Food and Clothing
Many churches already provide food and clothing closets for persons in crisis. Older adults can benefit from these provisions and can also find ways to serve by helping with these ministries.

Nursing Home Worship Services/Bible Studies
Seniors can provide music, testimonies, Scripture reading, prayers, Bible studies, and sermonettes in nursing homes on a weekly basis. Encourage team members to arrive early enough to visit the various halls and invite persons to come. Stay after the service for fellowship. Assist residents back to their rooms as needed.

Lunch Partner
A "lunch partner" has lunch weekly with a homebound person. Lunch may be brought into the home or the person taken out to eat. Eating on the same day each week gives the homebound individual a day to look forward to.

Meals On Wheels
Volunteers are needed to deliver meals. Contact the Senior Citizens Center or Area Council on Aging nearest you for information.

Transportation
People who do not drive must have assistance in getting to the doctor, dentist, grocery store, and other appointments. Even when available, taxi fares can become too much for limited budgets. Provide transportation to and from volunteer work for those who

don't have transportation. Transportation to churchwide events and senior adult functions is a way to begin a transportation ministry.

Reassurance Ministry

Develop a daily check-up or watch care service for senior citizens living alone. Use telephones, school bus drivers who watch for window signals, mail carriers, or a combination of these. A telephone caller has no obligation other than to check on their assigned person's well-being at a designated time each day.

Helping Hands

"Helping Hands" fix minor repairs for homebound individuals or senior adults who cannot financially arrange for a professional repairman. The senior volunteer works free, but materials are paid for by the person needing assistance. Other names are "Fix-it Teams" or "SMART" (Small Maintenance and Repair Teams).

Tape/literature Distribution

Blind and visually handicapped persons will appreciate the quarterly *Open Windows* cassette. Devotionals, Bible readings, and prayer suggestions are featured. The cassette is listed on the "Sunday School and Family Periodicals" section of the dated literature form from LifeWay Christian Resources. Those seniors who still read enjoy magazines, journals, quarterlies, and newsletters.

Senior Adult Day Care

Initially, senior adult day care seems a fairly simple way of offering families a respite from daily caring of the elderly. However, each state has a complex set of rules and regulations regarding licensing day care facilities. Churches might consider these alternate methods of meeting this growing need:

1. **Adult sitting service**—Volunteers in the local church offer this service two or three times a week for half a day. To avoid

licensing requirements, no meal is prepared and no medication or physical therapy is administered. Participants must be able to get around fairly well by themselves.

2. **Satellite day care center**–Work with a medical organization to establish a satellite location for an adult day care. Contract with the medical center for physical and occupational therapists, special diets, and meal preparation. This simplifies licensing requirements and allows the day center to have medical support.

   This option requires financial commitment from the church. Average costs per person per day range from $25 to $35*. If specialized care is offered, that figure increases. Tax credits and private insurance offer little assistance. Supplementing the cost through the church budget should be considered.

   *For further information, refer to "Adult Day Care and Personal Care Homes Run by Churches or Church Operated Non-Profit Organizations," 1988, Carolyn Hopper, Summer Institute for Gerontological Studies, Baylor University. Mrs. Hopper has done extensive research into the subject and is available for consultation. She can be contacted by mail at 585 Amberidge, Atlanta, Georgia, 30328 or by phone at 1-404-252-4541.

3. **County-sponsored day care**–First Baptist Church, Brandon, Florida, houses a senior adult day care, but Hillsborough County, Department of Aging Services, is financially responsible. The county rents two modular homes from the church, employs a staff, and manages the program. Write to Dr. W. D. Millican, Senior Adult Minister, First Baptist Church, 204 West Morgan Street, Brandon, Florida, 33511 or call 1-813-689-1204 for more information.

Benefits of Caring Services

Great joy comes from ministering to senior adults. The following quote captures this thought quite well:

While we learn from all with whom we minister, only senior adults have the wisdom that comes from length of days. As we share the journey of those who are moving toward the light, our own faith is increased, and we sense anew God's purpose for us for all our days—to glorify Him and to declare His love to the world.[9]

[1]April Thompson, "Signs of Hope: Untangling Chronic Illness and Depression," *Aging Today* 19.1 (January/February 1998): 14.

[2]Robert L. Sheffield, Compiler, *Equipping Deacons in Caring Skills,* Volume 2 (Nashville: Convention Press, 1988), 70-77.

[3]Barbara Deane, *Caring for Your Aging Parents: When Love Is Not Enough* (Colorado Springs: NavPress, 1989), 49. Used by permission of NavPress/Pinon Press. All rights reserved. For copies, call 1-800-366-7788.

[4]Ibid., 50.

[5]Ibid., 53-54.

[6]Ibid., 59.

[7]Ibid., 59.

[8]Homer D. Carter, *Equipping Deacons in Caring Skills* (Nashville: Convention Press, 1980), 46.

[9]James E. Hightower, Jr., Editor, *Caring for Folks from Birth to Death* (Nashville: Broadman Press, 1985), 143.

Chapter 6

Ministering Through Music

by Bill Bacon

How to Start a Senior Adult Choir
Organization of Your Choir
Characteristics of Senior Adult Choir Members
Characteristics of the Older Voice
The Rehearsal
Ministry Opportunities Through Music
Individual Talents and Specialty Groups
The 21st Century Senior Adult and Music

Can you imagine…choir rehearsal where everyone shows up early; section leaders calling their sections without being reminded; feeling exuberant after a rehearsal; the choir extremely disappointed because you cancelled practice; choir members more concerned about your state of mind than their own feelings following a bus breakdown; gratitude from your choir because they have an opportunity to publicly express their love for God; feeling truly loved by every member of your choir?

I don't have to just imagine these blessings because they are realities I experience from leading a senior adult choir. This chapter will help you as a pastor, church staff member, lay coordinator of senior adult work, or a senior adult Sunday School department director—as well as ministers of music—glimpse the advantages of a vibrant senior adult music ministry in your church. Although I am using my place of service as an example, these ideas can be adapted to your church program.

How to Start a Senior Adult Choir

Starting a senior adult choir will be simple if the interest is high. If there is no vision about what a choir can mean to your church, you must become that visionary and spark the interest. Here are some ideas that may help create the spark for a choir in your church.

Locate and invite an established and successful senior adult choir to sing for your church. They can lead in one of your regular worship services or sing at a luncheon or fellowship. Another method of creating interest and vision is to visit an associational or state senior adult choir festival. Take some of your key "fire starters" and just observe. They will have the opportunity to see choirs of all sizes and talents and visualize what they desire to accomplish.

Every fall week-long senior adult Chautauquas are held across the country. Guest choirs perform at the worship services, providing opportunity for your prospective choir members to observe a senior singing group in person. Find your key supporters, get them to a Chautauqua, and let their enthusiasm spread to others.

As you decide on a rehearsal time, keep in mind:

- Many elderly do not feel comfortable traveling at night or coming into an empty house after dark.
- Having a rehearsal just before or after a regular Bible study and worship time makes for a long day.
- Meet the same time each week so that appointments and medical visits can be planned in advance.

Once a rehearsal is scheduled, allow plenty of time to publicize the first meeting. Use the church newsletter, bulletins, announcement sheets, and the local newspaper to spread the word. Enlist senior adult department directors to promote it through Sunday School. The most influential and visible supporter will be the pastor through the pulpit and his weekly column.

Some may be skeptical about beginning a senior adult choir. A verbal, one-on-one invitation will be most effective with them. You will hear excuses such as, "I can't sing" or "I've never sung in a choir before." Assure individuals that the entire choir will be learning together, and they will fit right in. Later if you find they truly can't "carry a tune in a bucket," don't be alarmed. Your purpose is not to make a perfect sound but to make a joyful noise. You may have to ask some to make a little softer noise! If non-singers still want to be involved, utilize their abilities to write absentees, provide refreshments at the beginning of rehearsal, hand out or file music, or assist a handicapped member.

Remember some have never been in a choir before and did not grow up in a graded choir program. They may not improve as fast as others, but they will improve. Keep good, basic choral techniques before them; the sound will gradually improve. You will find that seniors' strongest attribute is expression. Don't get them so concerned about notes that they forget to smile. Keep the fun in singing praises to the Lord.

Select your accompanist carefully. Skills are important, but don't let these skills get in the way of ministry. The accompanist must evidence patience at all times. A sigh or roll of the eyes may be misinterpreted as impatience or disgust. Under no circumstances should this happen. Encouragement from you and from the accompanist is vital.

When choosing a rehearsal room, keep several things in mind. Parking should be within walking distance, on the same level as the rehearsal room, and handicap accessible. Good lighting and favorable acoustics need to be considered. Use a microphone so those with hearing loss can hear you.

Selecting literature for your first rehearsal can be tricky. Unless you know your choir will have strong leadership in all four sections, begin with unison or two- or three-part literature. Keep in mind that this will probably be the first choir rehearsal many of your members have ever attended. They will be uneasy and lack confidence. Starting with a four-part selection may scare them into running out the door. Begin with a familiar song to boost confidence.

Avoid new rhythms and harmonizations. A new song may be easier for them to learn than to relearn an altered familiar song. The range of the older voice is somewhat limited. Beginning sopranos struggle with anything higher than a top line F. Basses start fading below the bottom line G. Your choir's range may be less or greater, but this range is average.

Keep the subject matter of your music varied. Your choir will want to sing about more subjects than heaven! With correct planning, you will find that seniors can make a vibrant contribution to any worship theme. As their attendance and confidence grow, you will be able to use an abundance of both old and new selections.

Joy Makers respond to many of the old anthems that have been sitting dormant on my library shelves. You will find many selections in issues of *Gospel Choir* and *The Church Musician*. Southern Baptist Convention Press publishes *The Senior Musician*, which contains singable as well as challenging anthems of all styles. In addition, the *Heritage Hymnal* (1998) contains favorite hymns suggested by senior adults during Chautauquas.

A medley of familiar choruses—usually a favorite part of their music repertoire—offers a refreshing change. Let your choir tell you what they enjoy. When ordering literature, order enough so that everyone in your choir will have a copy. Eyesight limitations make sharing music with a neighbor difficult.

Strive for a performance date or goal to stimulate attendance. Hearing your choir for the first time will dictate scheduling your first performance. Singing for family and friends is quite different from singing before the church on Senior Adult Day. Choose that first appearance carefully.

Your church may not have enough senior adults to start a choir. Consider the idea of a community senior adult choir. Check for interest among other churches in combining to have a choir. Assistance may be found in the leadership of the other church families.

Organization of Your Choir

The following officer and committee responsibilities are taken directly from the *Joy Maker Handbook,* First Baptist Church, Clinton, Mississippi. Choir members prepared the handbook. These are just ideas not rules. Your choir may wish to create their own guidelines.

President—Preside at all meetings and rehearsals. Plan with the director, other officers, and committee chairmen for a smooth operating organization. Serve as ex officio member of all committees.

Vice-President—Preside in the absence of the president. Be supportive of the president and director. Serve as chairman of the group leaders.

Recording Secretary and Associate—Maintain an updated roster of the members. Check records of attendance. Keep other records as needed for the smooth operation of the group.

Treasurer—Collect, handle, and serve as custodian of all "kitty" monies (actually a hat that is passed a couple of times a month to replenish the treasury). Keep the organization informed about the financial status.

Librarian—Collect, handle, and serve as custodian of music under the leadership of the director.

Historian—Maintain records in a scrapbook for posterity.

Outreach—Keep Joy Makers aware of the need to enlarge the ministry. Visit in the homes of prospective members. Maintain a high visibility in all senior adult Sunday School departments. Display posters as they are needed.

Ministries—Under the leadership of the ministries chairman, deliver a potted plant to a Joy Maker who has lost an immediate family member—spouse, child, father, mother, brother, sister, daughter-in-law, son-in-law. Deliver a meal at a convenient time to a member or spouse of a member who has come home from the hospital. On the death of a Joy Maker, send a wreath (on a stand) in remembrance. Send cards to Joy Makers who are experiencing sadness or a special blessing. Also send cards to friends of Joy Makers in times of need. Members of the committee are assigned their duties by the chairman for different periods of time.

Public Relations—Serve as liaison to the church office for pertinent information. Mail to host churches the information to be used for publicity (articles/pictures). Prepare articles for the news media, both local and out of town.

Attire—Work with the director in deciding on the attire for the group. Assist the members in securing materials. Advise or assist members in making their outfits.

Group Leaders—Contact absentees and group members when necessary. Work closely with the ministries chairman regarding absences due to sickness, bereavement, and so forth.

Social—Work closely with the president and director in planning all social events. Chair social committee in delegating responsibilities such as time, place, food, decorations, clean-up, and program.

New officers are elected in September, and the outgoing president is responsible for keeping up with any changes that have been made in the roster. *The Joy Maker Handbook* is published each October with pride. The handbook includes a listing of the church music staff and their phone numbers, the general officers, group leaders, committees, an alphabetical listing of every member with phone number and address, honorary members (those who are no longer able to attend), the listing of each member by group, birthdays by month, job descriptions, Joy Maker highlights from the preceding year, a page dedicated to the memory of those who died in the preceding year, and a note from the director.

An organization such as the one I have described results from years of effort. Begin with one officer or two or three. Streamline the organization to meet your needs.

Characteristics of Senior Adult Choir Members

The following characteristics are accurate in general, although seniors are as diverse as any other age group.

1. Senior adults love and care for each other. An organization such as a choir can focus on the needs and concerns of its members. The ministries committee of my choir helps members experiencing difficulties with health, transportation, household chores, or bereavement. In addition, choir members are "prayer warriors." I count on them to faithfully lift up my concerns daily to our Lord.

2. Seniors have a strong bond with anyone who ministers to them. When I first started working with the Joy Makers ("Make a joyful noise to the rock of our salvation" Ps. 95:1, KJV), I wondered if my young age would make a difference in how they would respond to me. After the first rehearsal, I sensed a real love from them. The more I gave of myself, the more they gave of themselves. Before long a bond was created that will last forever. I'm sure I made many mistakes as their leader, but they overlooked my faults and praised my strong points. Their praise, though often embarrassing, has buoyed my confidence as a minister of music.

3. Seniors find security in organization and routine. Conversely, constant change in their comfort zone brings insecurity. Give your choir as much advance notice as possible when any changes are anticipated. A steady temperament from the choir leader also helps produce an orderly atmosphere.

4. Seniors enjoy fellowship. The Joy Makers take advantage of every opportunity to fellowship. A special birthday, a welcome-back party, or even a holiday party is reason enough to come to choir early. Allow for ample fellowship time before rehearsals begin.

Retreats are another excellent atmosphere for fellowship. At least once a year the choir and I spend a day together in a retreat setting, usually in preparation for a special program. This time is not only profitable musically but also a time to get to know new members. Annually the Joy Makers host a Christmas banquet. Upon entering the fellowship hall, each person is given a small stocking in which to place his or her Lottie Moon Christmas Offering. The total is proudly announced at the end of a short musical program.

Fellowship is a vital part of a successful senior adult music ministry. Encourage your group to plan creative social events.

5. Senior adults love to make new acquaintances and have new experiences. Encourage each choir member to be an outreach leader or ambassador for your choir. Surround the new members with love and support until they find their sense of belonging.

Although they like order and routine as mentioned, seniors also respond well to challenges. Whether you take them on a one-day trip to a place they have never been or introduce a new rehearsal technique, the response is usually positive.

6. Senior adults need communication. Whether in the form of a written note, phone call, or a verbal word, communication is essential. Physical handicaps such as hearing loss or sporadic short-term memory loss may affect some of your elderly members. Learn to repeat yourself, especially when communicating times, dates, and specific details about a future event. However, never talk down to any of your senior saints. They deserve all the respect you can give and will respect you in return.

Informative mailings to the entire choir are a great way of communicating. Use written handouts and the phone. The caller can pass on information and at the same time minister by a short conversation.

Another effective form of communication is one-on-one conversation. Most senior adults arrive at a scheduled function 30 to 40 minutes before it begins. Use this time to have personal conversations. Be sure you give the person your undivided attention with good eye contact. In public when you see one of your choir members, go out of your way to speak to him or her. Commit each name to memory and call each by name at every opportunity.

Characteristics of the Older Voice

As we look at the senior adult voice, it will be helpful to review the characteristics of all musical instruments. The sound produced is

99

the result of a power source, a vibration, and a resonator. The guitar's power source is the finger plucking the string, its vibration is the string itself, and the resonator is the wooden housing. The trumpet's power source is the air being blown through it, the vibration is the lips, and the resonator is the tubing.

The human voice, the most beautiful and flexible of God's instruments, possesses these same characteristics. The power source is the breath, the vibration is the vocal chords, and the resonator is the mouth, throat, and sinuses. Changes take place as the voice gets older. The lungs, which generate the power source, lose much of their elasticity and expansion is more difficult. The average senior adult cannot breathe as deep, sustain a phrase as long, or control the held note as well.

The vocal chords, which are responsible for the vibration, lose elasticity as well as muscle tone. Control is difficult; therefore, wobbles and heavy vibrato seem to take over. The throat and mouth, which make up the majority of the resonator, have their own set of problems. With the loss of elasticity, the mouth has more difficulty opening wide and expansion in the throat becomes more laborious. With these effects of aging, a perfect choral sound and blend is unlikely. I am thankful that God does not require a perfect sound—just the best "joyful noise" we can make.

If you are the director, keep your goals and expectations high. Letting your choir slide by with whatever sound is offered promotes laziness. Stress the importance of good posture at all times. Singing with energy in mind and body helps avoid many bad vocal habits. Dying phrases, singing Rs, and closing vowels prematurely are just a few indications of reduced energy.

The end result of this lack of energy is expressionless faces. Encourage choir members to let their faces communicate the message of the song. Age should not excuse laziness or lethargy. The director's duty is to remind the choir in a positive way to give their best to the Lord in all that they do.

The Rehearsal

Even though your first rehearsal has been mentioned earlier in the chapter, the following ideas may help establish a rehearsal routine. Allow me to personalize by describing a typical Thursday morning rehearsal with the Joy Makers.

The president of the choir calls the group to order as much as 15 minutes before the actual rehearsal begins. Our rehearsal begins at 10:30 so by 10:15 the president has begun. The choir knows to be ready and most of them are already in their seats. This preliminary time may be adjusted depending on the number of announcements to be made and business to consider.

At times a special birthday may be celebrated, with refreshments starting as early as 10:00. Usually this party is hosted by a family member, but our social committee is always ready to help. Make the choir aware of these special times so they can arrive early.

At 10:15 prayer concerns are voiced, followed by a devotional thought, poem, or a short reading. Announcements may consist of welcoming new members or visitors, passing the "kitty," discussing committee reports, birthdays, special recognitions, or telling a good joke. A hearty laugh will start any rehearsal on a bright note.

By 10:30 the microphone is turned over to the director. Our rehearsal room is rather large, and the microphone helps my voice carry. Physical warm-ups are not always needed; however, mild aerobic movement—arm swinging, walking in place, or head rolling—should energize the group.

Vocal warm-ups provide an excellent opportunity to work on posture, breathing, and a good, open sound. A simple vocalization is "Ma, Pa, and Baby Ned." Starting on an easy low note like C, sing ma-ma-ma-ma-ma rapidly. Move up a half step and sing pa-pa-pa-pa-pa, up another half step to ba-ba-ba-ba-ba, up to be-be-be-be-be, and finally up to ne-ne-ne-ne-ned. Continue to go up the scale but not too far. This exercise loosens the jaw, draws attention to crisp consonants, and encourages open vowels. To focus on a good placement of the power source, have your choir hiss like a snake. Repeat as loudly as possible. The muscles in the abdomen are the correct muscles to use in supporting the vocal sound. Take as much tension and pressure off the throat and jaw as possible.

Whether you are a trained musician or not, you must always strive to improve your choir's **sound.** Mini voice lessons are quite common in my rehearsals. Do not be too technical, and vary your approach with many different examples. I would like to say that the Joy Makers never sing Rs, always have open vowels, never ignore consonants, and always have great expression; but this is not always true. After many years and many rehearsals, we still make mistakes. Does that mean give up? No. Continue to strive for perfection, because the Lord deserves our best.

What about **breathing?** Here is a humorous example that has worked well for me: Get your choir to visualize their bodies or lungs as giant barrels. A giant barrel may be easier for some to identify with than others, but the image usually brings a chuckle. Tell them they are filling the barrel with water from the top. This is the sensation one feels when filling his lungs with air. Even though their lungs have lost some of the elasticity, breathing exercises will improve control.

Good posture will also contribute to correct breathing. Get them to picture their windpipes as water hoses. To stop the flow of water you have two options. Turn it off or put a crimp in it. Many singers put a crimp in their air flow by using poor posture. The back should be as straight as possible with the chest up but not out. Shoulders should be down and relaxed not pulled back. A good demonstration to find this correct positioning is to have the choir stand, lift their arms over their heads, and slowly lower them keeping their chests in the position they were in when their arms were over their heads. As the shoulders fall let them be totally relaxed with arms by their sides. This posture should be ideal both for sitting and standing.

A good **choral sound** requires blended voices. To achieve this blend the sense of hearing must be keen from the inner ear and the outer ear. Hearing yourself and those around you is essential. With senior adults the slight loss of hearing is common. Most of your uncertain singers are well aware that they are not singing the same as everyone else, and you rarely hear them. If a choir member is singing louder than everyone else, never call attention to him in public. He probably doesn't realize that he is singing loudly and would appreciate your telling him about it in private. Just a look from then on will let him know when to sing softer.

Visual examples are always helpful when giving a mini voice lesson or describing the sound you are striving for. Having your choir yawn lets them feel the open sensation in the mouth and throat. Make sure there is plenty of circulating air in the room. Vowel sounds ideally need to all sound alike. An up and down or north and south vowel is much preferred over an east and west vowel. A simple up and down motion with your hand in front of your mouth cues everyone to think north and south. To remind your choir to fill up their barrels from the top, pull your hands apart in front of your diaphragm. Your body language and expression communicate volumes. Create your own reminders that you can use even in the middle of a concert.

Bad phrasing may arise if you do not keep listening for it. Breathing limitations can play havoc with a good phrase. Don't let your choir get into the bad habit of breathing when they feel like it. Alert them to the message and thought they are trying to relate in the song. Breathing exercises should be encouraged not only in rehearsal but also in the leisure of their homes.

Does the senior adult choir need to sing from **memory?** The answer to this question has been debated many times. The Joy Makers rarely sing with music and take great pride in singing without it. You may hear excuses such as, "I'm too old to memorize" or "I just can't memorize like I used to." I have found that senior adults can memorize but not as fast as they once did. As I direct, I mouth the words to assist them.

In **closing the rehearsal,** leave on a good note. Sing something familiar that everyone enjoys—a theme song, hymn, or a good singable chorus. Don't forget to compliment the choir on the positive things they have sung and done. A pat on the back goes a long way. Let them leave feeling good about the choir and themselves.

Ministry Opportunities Through Music

The reputation of your choir and their eagerness to share the gospel will spread rapidly to others. Be prepared for invitations from other organizations in the community. Given enough notice, most of your choir can take a short excursion to perform for others. You may be invited to share a program at another senior adult luncheon, nursing home, retirement village, or possibly a worship service in a sister church.

When your choir has been invited to present a concert, prepare ahead of time to avoid time loss and confusion.

- At least an hour before the performance, rehearse in the room where the concert will be presented to give your choir a chance to feel more comfortable and confident.
- Make sure everyone can see the director, hear the piano, and hear each other.
- Establish good eye contact between the pianist and director.
- Have a seat for everyone. Senior adults cannot stand for an extended time and must sit periodically.
- Place the strongest singers in the middle of each section. They will vocally encourage those around them.
- Microphones should be easily accessible to the users, and a microphone check is advised for every speaker and soloist.
- Never put someone in an embarrassing position that could be detrimental to your program, to your ministry, or to the individual. Be safe not sorry.

- Never force anyone to sing a solo, but encourage anyone who possesses the talent.

How long should the concert last? Thirty minutes is long enough. Coupled with introductions to the songs and any other special music such as a quartet, trio, vocal solo, piano solo, handbell selection, or maybe a reading, the entire program may last an hour. Never overstay your welcome; leave them wanting more.

During the program give the choir president an opportunity to thank the host church and bring greetings from your church family. Giving personal statistics, such as the age of the oldest choir member, age of the youngest choir member, the year the choir originated, and the number of members enrolled will add interest to the program. Never mention a name with these statistics unless you clear it with the individual first.

Involve as many people as possible in the program. Some may sing, and others may have the gift of speech. Have a member introduce the different choral selections. If you are concerned about what they might say, write it out in advance to give them an opportunity to learn it.

Avoid a processional into the choir loft. The congregation can become very uneasy while watching a senior adult move slowly up and down steps. A fall would be tragic, so never put one of your members in a position to hurry. Be seated 15 minutes prior to the start of the program. Allow plenty of time for the choir to have a rest room break before the concert begins. Comfort will allow them to be fully attentive to the music. Avoid bright lights if possible. Senior eyes are more sensitive, and a squint is often misinterpreted as a frown. A good percentage of your members wear glasses, and the glare can be distracting for the singer and worshiper.

The question of whether or not to take a choir on tour should be carefully considered. The biggest fear might be taking the elderly away from their homes, medical care, and families. Even though senior adults may be a bit more fragile, they are well aware of their limitations and what they can and cannot do. If a member tells you it would be best for him not to go on an overnight trip, respect his decision. Don't try to talk him into doing something you may regret later. Assure him the choir will be making shorter trips also.

Most of your choir will be eager to travel. Make sure you inform them about the trip months in advance and communicate such things as destination, dates, cost, transportation, and accommodations. They can adjust their schedules if enough information is given early.

When planning a choir trip, select the music you wish to perform and decide on a destination. Involve your officers or the entire choir for suggestions. Travel time and length of the trip may limit your destination. Take advantage of contacts you have in different parts of the country. One of your fellow travelers may have a family member or friend who would like for you to sing at her church. A Chautauqua or senior adult convention will often determine your travel direction. Once the destination is decided, gather information about the area and all attractions along the way.

What about the length of your trip? Early in my ministry I took a suggestion from a group of my younger retirees and took a 10-day tour. Before the trip was over, I found I had made a mistake. The last few days were very tiring for all.

Since that time I have taken more than 12 singing trips, and the following schedule works best for us. Leave on Sunday morning and return on Wednesday evening. Counting a homecoming concert the following Sunday, we usually present up to five concerts: two on Sunday, one on Monday morning, and one on Wednesday evening. We do a lot of singing, have plenty of fun, and are away from home three nights.

Take advantage of regular worship schedules when you are singing in another church. Attendance on a weekday night will be discouraging. Between Sunday and Wednesday, the choir can see the sights and enjoy fellowship with each other.

Plan your activities ahead of time if possible. My choir always wants a detailed itinerary given to them well in advance of our departure. Remember, senior adults are more comfortable with order and direction. Be sure to find out the cost, tour times, and business hours of all attractions visited.

Accommodations can also be taken care of many weeks in advance. With youth and young adults you may choose to stay in homes of the host church. However, with senior adults safety must be your primary concern. Elderly guests in the home may not be able to negotiate stairs or find their way down a dark hallway to the bathroom. A motel room with two occupants works well. Give your choir opportunity to sign up for roommates weeks in advance.

Detailed information about planning senior adult trips is given in chapter 8 on pages 148-154. The suggestions found there apply to senior adult choirs as well. The expense of chaperones, accompanists, and director need to be included in the fixed amount charged. After this figure is totaled and divided by the number of choir members going, you have your cost per individual. The only other expenses will be meals, snacks, souvenirs, and optional attractions. Make everyone aware of these other expenses well before departure.

A tour booklet or itinerary sheet will be helpful for each person. Remember that seniors like order, and they respond well to seeing when and where they are going next. Phone numbers, addresses, and contact persons are important facts that can be given to family members and friends before departure. This also gives those remaining at home specific places and activities for prayer.

Publicity for your trip will be quite helpful to the host church. A black and white photograph taken six weeks ahead of time will come in handy when preparing posters, programs, and biographical information. Compose a prepared news release about your choir including the date, time, location of the program, and summary about the choir. Keep in mind that the release may be read in a local newspaper as well as church newsletters. The photograph of the choir should accompany the release. The following is an announcement prepared for the Joy Makers.

> The Joy Makers of First Baptist Church, Clinton, Mississippi, will be in concert on (day, date, time, location). The 65-voice senior adult choir is directed by Bill Bacon, Minister of Music. The Joy Makers have toured in most of the southern states and have presented over 50 concerts in churches and assemblies. They have been the featured choir at Ridgecrest Baptist Assembly and the Southern Baptist Church Music Conference. The program consists of anthems, gospel music, hymn arrangements, a gospel quartet, and the Joy Bells handbell choir. There is no charge and the public is invited to attend.

Three weeks prior to the concert, a poster with time, place, location, and picture should also be mailed to the host church.

The printed program for the audience must be prepared before departure also. On the front cover of each program we use an original logo created by a member of our church family. The inside of the program includes the order of worship, a listing of the choir members, soloists, narrators, choir officers, church staff, the tour itinerary, and a short history of the choir and church. Be sure to prepare enough programs for all of your concerts. One responsible person can be in charge of placing the programs in the foyer and collecting those left over at the close of the performance.

Take numerous photographs on the trip. If you don't feel confident with your skills in this area, get someone to do it for you. The more photographers you have the better. Encourage at least one person to take slides or a video, if you have the capability. The choir historian will be able to use some photos in the choir scrapbook and, if a trip log is kept, photos can be included. The slides or video can be used at a fellowship after your return. Following the homecoming concert, a party with friends and family members offers a great opportunity to share the wonderful experiences. Invite prospective members to join you at the party.

Individual Talents and Specialty Groups

After working with your senior adults for awhile, you will begin to discover a wealth of talents that some didn't even know they possess. One obvious musical talent is a good singing voice for a solo, part of a trio, quartet, sextet, or even an ensemble. Even though you basically give voice lessons each week in rehearsal, there may arise an opportunity to offer vocal instruction to an individual who wants to enhance his or her vocal talent. If you do not feel that you have the gifts or knowledge to work with someone privately, find a competent voice teacher.

God can use talents other than singing. One gentleman in my choir periodically plays his harmonica for the devotion time at the beginning of choir. A lady who has a difficult time with her memory still plays the piano as well as she did 20 years ago. One man played the guitar to accompany a gospel selection in our program; he could also fiddle. Harold, almost 90 years old, has recited from memory 10-minute dramatic readings. Maybe a "Harold" in your church could be an effective addition to one of your musical programs by reading or telling a personal story that amplifies a song.

Group activities you may wish to explore musically are handbells, dulcimers, ukuleles, and kazoos. Some of my senior adult choir members expressed an interest in ringing handbells and, as a result, the Joy Bells were formed. Of the 12 ringers who showed up for the first rehearsal, only three could read music. One of the three quit after two weeks because patience was not one of her virtues. The other two stuck with it and the year was filled with teaching the basic ABCs of music. They learned note values, key signatures, and how to keep a beat. Many rehearsals saw little use of the handbells.

The group rehearsed for one year and made their first public appearance at a Joy Maker choir rehearsal. They made many mistakes, but we were all proud. They gradually improved and now make regular appearances at our Wednesday prayer meetings. Confidence grows each time we perform. The fellowship and mental challenge has brought us much closer to each other. Members take their roles seriously and let me know well in advance when they are going to be absent. Regular substitutes are on standby.

A dulcimer class is taught at many of the Chautauquas scheduled around the country. A sister church in our community formed a dulcimer choir that rehearses twice a week. They have 15 members and perform at numerous gatherings around our city. As with our handbell choir, they have a strong sense of commitment and dedication as well as camaraderie.

Ukuleles are a popular instrument to play in a group as are kazoos. I have even heard a kazoo choir play "In the Garden." Let the talents and creativity of your choir lead to other specialty groups.

The 21st Century Senior Adult and Music

As I look into the 21st century I do so with excitement and a strong personal interest. At this writing I am 51. In 15 years I will be able to draw full social security. I still play competitive basketball, softball, racquetball, swim three miles a week, and regularly shoot in the high 70s on the links.

I am like many other men and women in my age group who are taking better care of themselves through exercise and proper diet. What does this mean? Barring tragedy, I will more than likely experience a full, active, and longer life than the average senior adult of today. The younger generation of senior adults is living longer. They are becoming more health-conscious by eating proper foods and exercising. In recent years they have become more aware of certain dangers to the body such as tobacco, alcohol, overeating, and lack of exercise. By avoiding these dangers, senior adults are avoiding many health problems. These factors, coupled with the advances in medical technology, are adding more productive years to their lives. Therefore, you can expect a more active and energetic generation of senior adults. What are the implications for music? Healthier, physically fit seniors of the future may produce a more pleasing vocal sound.

By the year 2015 more seniors will be trained musically. Most senior adults today were never in a graded choir program or youth choir. You will see music that is more challenging with a greater emphasis on specialty groups. Instrumental ensembles, brass quintets, rock-and-roll Christian bands, handbells, recorder choirs, and wind ensembles will probably be common. These groups will want to be challenged musically.

Choirs will reflect the different age groups within the senior adult years. Choirs for younger, middle, and older seniors may replace the "one size fits all" senior adult choir of today. The Junior Senior Choir and the Senior Senior Choir may take turns filling the choir loft! Will there be a choir loft? Who knows? I pray that if it is God's will, I will be right in the middle of it!

Senior adult choirs and ensembles will still enjoy the music of their youth. I discovered this principle 15 years ago when my wife and I prepared a Nelson Eddy and Jeanette McDonald Valentine's Day program for our senior adults. They commented on the fond memories it recalled. This past Valentine's Day we were invited to present a musical program and thought it would be a good idea to resurrect the same songs. This time we even added period costumes. Comments after the program were, "I remember those songs because my parents sang them to me," and "Next time throw in a little 'Sentimental Journey.'" Times change—even in 15 years.

The senior adult of 2015 will probably love music from "Good News", "Lightshine", and "Celebrate Life." I foresee someone compiling a senior adult musical with folk songs from the 60s and 70s. What about the 50-year-old man in 2035 who responds to the praise service with the use of drums, synthesizer, and electric bass and guitar. In 2050 will he still need that to effectively worship? What will be the musical styles of the youth in that year? Will the pendulum swing back to a more traditional style of worship? Whatever the style then, we seniors will still probably gravitate to the music we grew up with.

Senior adult choirs of the future will probably be more ministry-oriented than performance-oriented. Boomers like to get out in the world and make a difference. Groups may prefer singing in a busy mall to singing for a Sunday evening worship service. Choir trips will combine missions and ministry opportunities with singing and worship.

Membership in senior choirs will be fluid, with some seniors living two or more places at various times of the year. With less emphasis on retirement and more emphasis on moving into and out of careers, seniors will have periods of work and periods of leisure. Rehearsal "seasons" may replace year-round rehearsals.

Friendships and personal care will continue to motivate participation in senior adult choirs. With the loss of extended family living nearby, and with more mobility, seniors will move into their older years with fewer long-term friendships. Church will continue to be the place they look to for "family."

My prayer is that as a senior adult in someone else's choir, I will have the spiritual qualities, wisdom, and temperament of the average senior adult today. Their constant encouragement, support, and love sustain me and give me the desire to continue in God's will. If you are contemplating the beginning of a senior adult choir in your church, I encourage you to do so today. You will be putting yourself in a position to receive immeasurable blessings.

Chapter 7

Senior Adults on Mission

by Loren Williams

**The Message of Missions
The Motivation for Missions
The Methods of Missions
Enlisting Today's Seniors in Missions
Enlisting Younger Seniors in Missions
Helping Senior Adults Become Volunteers**

From Genesis to Revelation the Bible is a missionary book. God continues to ask today the timeless question He posed to Isaiah: "Whom shall I send? And who will go for us?" (Isa. 6:8). Thousands of senior adults have responded to this call through volunteer mission opportunities. Those who serve describe their experiences as "life-changing," "the capstone of our service to the Lord," grateful that "others see how Jesus works through us."

In this chapter we will overview volunteer missions–short-term and long-term, local, national, and international–in order to demonstrate the many ways God is using seniors to extend His kingdom. With the growing numbers of active, healthy seniors entering their retirement years, volunteer missions has a bright future. How can your church participate? What blessings will result from becoming involved in God's mission enterprise?

The Message of Missions

Missions is cooperating with God to extend His kingdom in the world. Missions began in the heart of God. "For God so loved the world, that he gave his only begotten Son, that whosoever believeth in him should not perish, but have everlasting life" (John 3:16, KJV). He continues to call His listening children to trust Him and step out in faith. Paul expressed the thrill that many of us have felt when he said, "We are God's fellow workers" (1 Cor. 3:9). "Missions is not man's scheme for influencing the world but God's purpose and plan for redeeming it."[1]

Every Christian is called to be on mission with God. Some have quietly obeyed while others have shown a reluctance to get involved. Not every Christian is called as a vocational missionary, but we are all called to be on mission where God places us. The Holy Spirit guides us to identify ways of sharing God's care and concern. Being on mission may mean getting involved in your own community, in the neighborhood across town, in another city, in your own state, throughout the nation, or around the world. This call is to persons of all ages.

The Motivation for Missions

As I have worked with senior adults for the last 20 years, I have found most of them mission-minded. However, many have let their interest in and concern for missions be confined to praying for missions and giving their money through special offerings and the Cooperative Program. These important activities should continue. However, my heart's desire is to see senior adults become personally involved in volunteer missions.

Perhaps the most important element in being a volunteer in missions is a desire to be used of God. Coupled with a willingness to follow His leadership, wonderful and unexpected things begin to happen.

Why do seniors make good missions volunteers? They have
- resources of time and money to use at their own discretion
- expertise and experience in many areas of service
- a desire to invest in the Lord's work

- a willingness to take chances and a spirit of adventure
- caring hearts concerning the needs of others and a desire to be useful

Why do many of them volunteer?

- God called them to missions when they were young, but because of many circumstances they were unable to go.
- Some were saved in their adult years and now feel called to commit themselves for missions.
- Others developed a recent awareness of mission needs.
- They were enlisted by another volunteer who shared the joy in volunteering and challenged them to pray about their involvement.
- They were looking for a new challenge.
- They have a love for the Lord and desire to share their faith.

Not all seniors hear the call to missions involvement. Some of the reasons senior adults give for not volunteering for missions are valid; others are expressions of fear or merely excuses. Here are some that I have encountered.

- don't feel qualified
- don't want to be gone from home
- too many other obligations
- adult children or grandchildren to care for
- poor health
- lack the necessary income
- have already served my time in volunteering
- needed here at my local church

Become aware of the many volunteer opportunities for senior adults and know how to help them get involved.

The Methods of Missions

Some ministries are designed for individuals, some for couples, some for small or large groups, while others are for families or intergenerational groups. We will look at mission opportunities on

115

the local church field, in the association, through state conventions, the North American Mission Board (NAMB), International Mission Board (IMB), and several agencies and organizations where volunteers serve. As you read, notice how many methods God uses to get His message to the lost.

Community and State Missions
Local Church

A group of seniors in a Houston, Texas, church staffed a summer school lunch program. As they met the students who came daily for their sack lunches, they became aware that God had placed the church across the street from an elementary school for a purpose. They began to pray about the needs in the school. Out of their concern, a tutoring ministry began. Boys and girls were selected by the principal to stay after school one afternoon a week for table games, refreshments, and help with homework. Friendships across the age span were formed as the seniors showed Christ's love in a tangible way to the community.

William Tanner, former president of the Home Mission Board (now NAMB), said: "Missions is touching in the name of Jesus Christ the needs of a person next door or thousands of miles away across the ocean."[2] This statement echoes the message of Jesus that we are to be witnesses in Jerusalem or right where we are. Some have the idea that they must go long distances to be involved in missions. But the New Testament teaches we must begin at home and face-to-face.

Charles Roesel of First Baptist Church, Leesburg, Florida, has coined a phrase describing missions at the home base—ministry evangelism. He says, "Ministry evangelism is simply caring for persons in the name of Jesus Christ. It is meeting persons at the point of their need and ministering to them physically and spiritually. The intent of ministry evangelism is to present the good news of God's love in order to introduce persons to Jesus."[3]

Steve Sjogren calls community missions servant evangelism. He defines it as "demonstrating the kindness of God by offering to do some act of humble service with no strings attached."[4]

The following list may stimulate you to think of other mission opportunities that exist in your community:

Literacy	English as a second language
Tutoring	Latchkey ministry
Jail or prison ministry	Ministry to families of prisoners
Homeless shelters	Battered wives shelters
Persons with AIDS/families	Nursing Homes
Senior Adult Day Care	Used furniture ministry
Used health equipment	Resort ministry

Refer to the list of recommended reading and other resources at the end of the chapter. (See pp. 174-177 for additional ministry ideas.)

Local Baptist Association

Denton Baptist Association in Denton, Texas, houses a clothing room that serves the entire community. Volunteers sort and label the clothes and staff the facility. Most of the associations in the Southern Baptist Convention have a list of volunteer mission opportunities. Needs that can be met by senior adults usually top the list. Contact your local Director of Missions for more information.

Baptist State Conventions

Ask your state convention office for a list of ministry and mission opportunities available to senior adult groups. Examples include disaster relief, construction crews, river ministry, partnership missions with other states and overseas, office volunteers, youth camps, resort ministries, and criminal justice ministry.

National Missions

Members of a senior adult Sunday School class went to Pascagoula, Mississippi, to work with a truckers ministry. Gene and Barbara

Brown had this to say about the trip: "We felt the local people who put so much of themselves into this wonderful work were encouraged by the presence of seniors who cared enough to drive 600 miles to work side by side with them." The group conducted Vacation Bible Schools in two projects and did repair and painting work as well.

A group of seniors from Texas travelled to Jefferson City, Tennessee, to minister to persons in poverty. After they returned home, they led their church to provide money to drill a well and septic tank for a needy family.

These examples illustrate the impact seniors can have beyond the borders of their states. The North American Mission Board (NAMB) of the Southern Baptist Convention has a number of volunteer mission opportunities. For information on those listed below, write to NAMB, Adult Mobilization Unit, 4200 North Point Parkway, Alpharetta, GA 30022-4176 or call 1-800-462-VOLS.

Mission Service Corps

Volunteers pay their own expenses and serve full-time from four months up to two years in home missions and evangelism. About three-fourths of all volunteers assigned are laypersons. Approximately one-third are senior adults. Occasionally volunteers receive small stipends or housing.

Opportunities for service through MSC are unlimited. Seniors with certain job skills are needed in the fields of medicine, construction, administration, computers, education, music, library science, finance, and secretarial services.

Other jobs do not require previous experience but utilize on-the-job training. These include taking surveys, Vacation Bible Schools, Backyard Bible Clubs, Bible studies, outreach, community ministries, youth, crisis ministry, literacy, English as a second language, apartment ministry, after-school care, nursing home ministries, evangelism, food service, homebound ministries, and maintenance.

Seniors may serve as missions directors for a local church, association or state office, or as Mission Service Corps consultants.

Many of the assignments require living in another city and/or state. There is no age limit. Qualifications include a genuine salvation experience, active membership in a Southern Baptist church, flexibility, adaptability, willingness to share skills in mission service, maturity, dedication, good physical and emotional health, and financial resources to provide support, including transportation and lodging if necessary. An orientation program is required.

Tentmakers, MSC

Adults, couples, and families may serve from four months or longer as Tentmakers. They must provide for their living expenses through marketplace (secular) employment as part of this program.

Ministry opportunities are varied and as numerous as one's imagination. Positions are available in church planting, pastoring, student ministry, associational work, and church staffs. If someone feels called to nontraditional, creative ministry, the MSC office assists the person in finding a ministry location to fulfill that calling.

Tentmakers must be able to commit to the time of service needed, have Southern Baptist church endorsement, and provide solid references. Education, experience, and other requirements are determined by the individual field requirements.

Short-term Mission Volunteers

Individuals, couples, families, and groups who serve from one week to four months are responsible for all personal expenses in this ministry. Opportunities for service include approximately 300 construction projects each year. They range from minor repairs to new construction. Volunteer construction crews require both skilled and unskilled labor, since each skilled worker ideally needs three to four helpers.

Non-construction projects include camp ministries; church

119

growth through witnessing and visiting; cooking for shelters and camps; evangelism; general maintenance; houseparenting; interim pastorates; medical, dental, nursing, resort, seaman's and migrant ministry; mission centers; special events; secretarial and clerical work; surveys, youth work; music; Vacation Bible Schools; and Backyard Bible Clubs.

Qualifications are the same as MSC volunteers; however, orientation is not required. Groups can serve anytime during the year, but there are more projects during the summer. Groups pay their own expenses.

Campers on Mission

Camping provides many opportunities for ministry and witness, and Christian campers of all ages and types can grow together through fellowship, training, and service. Campers on Mission is a national fellowship of Christian campers who desire to share their faith with others.

Some of the features of COM are free membership, American Bible Society Scripture portions, national newsletter, membership packet, area chapters, and a national rally each year in June. COM is composed of Christian campers of many denominations who see themselves "on mission" wherever they go. There is no age limit.

Senior Adult World Changers

World Changers offers hands-on, one-week missions experiences in a prepackaged approach where all the logistics of lodging, meals, schedules, construction, ministry, and worship are pre-arranged.

World Changers partners with community agencies, associations of churches, state conventions, ministry centers, and local churches to meet needs in a community. This approach reflects a deliberate choice to maximize the witness for Christ and extend the impact of the week.

Whether it is crossing racial, socio-economic, or denominational lines, World Changers seek to build bridges with the gospel. Participants must pay a registration fee which covers all lodging expenses, meals, and needed materials.

National Fellowship for Baptists in Missions (NFBM)
These are affinity groups that organize for fellowship and service. Each group will use its skill or interest as a means of service and witness. Some of the groups include Senior Partners who are senior adults interested in church starting and church planting. Others include medical/dental fellowships, educator fellowships, and various other group support missions. All volunteers pay all expenses.

Disaster Relief
Volunteers serve in time of disaster in many different ways. Training and enlistments for disaster relief are coordinated through each State Convention. Service opportunities include mass care and feeding, clean-up, damage assessment, child care, and long-term rebuild. Volunteers work with the American Red Cross and FEMA. Volunteers pay all expenses required to serve.

International Missions
Following their retirement, Jim and Janet Palmer served in Nicaragua, where he pastored a church and she taught English in a church school. Russell and Nadine Wills heard God's call to missions many years ago but were unable to go until recently. They have completed assignments in Mexico and Costa Rica. Ralph and Waldene Shuman have served in Tanzania doing maintenance, office and electrical work, leading Bible studies, and teaching English.

The International Mission Board of the Southern Baptist Convention coordinates volunteer missions assignments overseas. For information on the opportunities listed below write to IMB, P. O. Box 6767, Richmond, VA 23230 or call 1-800-888-8657.

Volunteers in Missions

Short-term assignments are coordinated by a Southern Baptist missionary and do not require a foreign language. They last an average of one week to four months. There is no age limit, nor is a physical exam required. Participants provide complete funding for air travel, field transportation, lodging, and meals. Overseas travel insurance at a nominal cost is required.

To qualify, volunteers should be a member of a Southern Baptist church, raise funds to pay expenses, have a skill or ability the missionaries are requesting from the field, be available during the time needed, and be willing to go wherever needed.

Some of the projects are revivals, witnessing, sports, community health, hunger and water relief, disaster response, church construction, emergency repairs, discipleship, leadership conferences, stewardship promotion, and church planting. Some of the specialized skills needed are those of physicians, nurses, dentists, paramedics, and English teachers.

Partnership Missions

A number of states have formed partnerships with a particular country and have a variety of projects for which they are recruiting. Contact your state office for information. Some of the conventions that have partnerships include Alabama, Arkansas, California, Florida, Georgia, Indiana, Kansas-Nebraska, Kentucky, Maryland-Delaware, Mississippi, Missouri, North Carolina, New England, Ohio, Oklahoma, South Carolina, Tennessee, Texas, Virginia, and Wyoming.

Partnership Evangelism

Pastor-led teams from SBC churches are linked with churches overseas for one- to two-week evangelistic campaigns. The pastor/team leader enlists the team and helps them with spiritual preparation and orientation. Primary requirements are a personal commitment to Jesus Christ, a willingness to work, readiness to witness, and flexibility. Volunteers must pay their own expenses.

International Service Corps

Open to individuals who acknowledge God's leading and are willing to serve 4 to 24 months to meet priority needs. ISC volunteers fill requests from career missionaries for teachers, youth workers, health care professionals, agriculturists, publication workers, and other critical assignments.

To qualify, a volunteer should be skilled or have the experience to match the job request, at least 21 years of age, a citizen or permanent resident of the United States, and an active member of a Southern Baptist church for at least 2 years. Limited funds are available from the IMB for needs-based situations.

Other Agencies

The following agencies work with Southern Baptists and our mission-sending organizations.

Woman's Missionary Union has a program called Volunteer Connection, a network which identifies needs and resources—both national and international—and matches them with a qualified volunteer. Through the Volunteer Connection program, individuals learn to extend their witness and ministry beyond themselves and their churches to fulfill the Great Commission.

Who can volunteer? Woman's Missionary Union defines a volunteer as a Christian who has felt the call to volunteer for mission service and has chosen to give his time, skills, and resources to meet a need in a mission setting.

Some identified needs are health care, child care, teaching, construction, maintenance, evangelism, and Vacation Bible Schools. A representative program is the Mississippi River Ministry, which reaches 143 counties or parishes in 7 states including Arkansas, Illinois, Kentucky, Louisiana, Mississippi, Missouri, and Tennessee.

Training involves individual or group studies and participation in a local church ministry. For more information write to Volunteer Connection, WMU, P.O. Box 830010, Birmingham, AL 35283-0010, call 1-205-991-4097, or email volconnection@wmu.org.

International Crusades, an evangelistic association, serves Southern Baptist churches as a consultant for church-to-church partnership evangelism. It works in cooperation with the IMB. Volunteer project numbers are assigned by the IMB. Baptist congregations overseas make the requests. Witnessing and preaching are the primary tools of evangelism. A team consists of a preacher and three to five laypersons. There is no age limit. Each team is responsible for all expenses. For more information write to International Crusades, Inc., 500 South Ervay #409A, Dallas, TX 75201, call 1-214-747-1444, or email intcrusade@aol.com. You may also contact their website at www.crusades.com.

Appalachian Outreach, a Christian poverty relief ministry, is composed of several ministries: a home repair ministry, a homeless shelter for families and single women called Samaritan House, a used-furniture ministry, and a community food pantry. Begun by Carson Newman College in Jefferson City, Tennessee, it cooperates with the local association, Tennessee Baptist Convention, and North American Mission Board. Volunteers are responsible for their expenses. Groups or individuals may participate one week or several months. There is no age limit. For more information write to Appalachian Outreach, 130 West Old A.J. Highway, Jefferson City, TN 37760 or call 1-423-475-5611.

Dr. Harry Fowler directs *Adults on Mission* in cooperation with NAMB. Volunteers work with children, in retirement centers, in homeless shelters, and at construction and mission centers. For more information write to Adults on Mission, P.O. Box 2095, Rocky Mount, NC 27802 or call 1-800-299-0385.

The Annuity Board of the SBC has provided an opportunity to individuals or groups to adopt a retired Baptist pastor or worker and spouse through *Adopt an Annuitant.* Many hundreds of these servants of the Lord are receiving $200 or less per month in annuity retirement income. Volunteers can adopt an annuitant for $75 per month or $900 per year. For more information write to Adopt an Annuitant, Annuity Board, SBC, P.O. Box 2190, Dallas, TX 75221-2190 or call 1-800-262-0511.

Missions Our Mission is a non-profit corporation with a global commitment that was begun by Dr. and Mrs. Taylor Henley in connection with IMB. Mission teams accompany Dr. and Mrs. Henley throughout the year to various places, such as India, Wales, Kenya, Peru, Singapore, Taiwan, Mexico, Hong Kong, and the Ukraine. Volunteers are enlisted to work in the Crimea and Odessa regions of Russia with evangelistic services, hospital visits, services in military posts, on the beaches, in the parks, shops, medical and dental clinics, therapy sessions, drug and alcohol abuse clinics, and with marriage and family life seminars. For more information write to Missions Our Mission, 902 North Main, #49, San Angelo, TX 76903 or call 1-800-633-2913.

Enlisting Today's Seniors in Missions

Although I am a senior adult, many volunteers in ministry with whom I am acquainted are from 10 to 20 years older than I. These older seniors have a commitment and concern for ministry which challenges other generations. They have been referred to as Power-Builders by Louis B. Hanks in his book *Vision, Variety, and Vitality.*

> PowerBuilders are the most mission-minded generation in the twentieth century.... They have a wealth of experience to offer, and their can-do spirit can be tapped for a multitude of projects and ministries.[5]

Declining health and limited financial resources keep some of this generation from volunteering for missions. However, many do, and they make a significant contribution both here and overseas. Those who cannot physically participate can be challenged to become prayer warriors for other volunteers and mission endeavors.

Hanks refers to my generation, those born between 1926 and 1944, as the PeaceMaker generation. He says this generation seeks to bring about peace between the generations that surround them. Many in this generation are investing themselves in the lives of their grandchildren. Others are caring for their parents who are still living. Some of this generation find themselves caring for adult children who have never left home or who have returned home.

Because of early retirement due to downsizing and buyouts, many PeaceMakers are leaving the job market and have much leisure time. Many have looked forward with great anticipation to retirement. When they have spent a few months resting, traveling, and catching up on home projects, they are ripe for involvement in voluntary missions and ministries. If they can be challenged by the many opportunities for volunteer ministry, their lives can take on a whole new meaning.

In his book *Three Generations,* Gary L. McIntosh refers to this generation as Builders. He characterizes them as hard workers, savers, frugal, patriotic, loyal, private, cautious, respectful, dependable, stable, and tolerant. In describing their religious characteristics, he says they are committed to the church, support foreign missions, enjoy Bible study, are loyal to their denomination, minister out of obligation, and worship in reverence.[6]

McIntosh says, "Builders will find the aging process less traumatic if they find meaningful and challenging ways of using their time. Churches can have a major role in helping Builders find places of service."[7]

Enlisting Younger Seniors in Missions

The generation coming along behind me is known as baby boomers. Hanks refers to them as the PathFinder generation–those born between the years 1945 and 1964. The older segment of this generation has been referred to as educated, rebellious, independent, affluent, and strong-willed. They are not as committed to the church or to their employers as were their parents. Though many of them have dropped out of the institutional churches of their youth, they are searching for spiritual meaning and fulfillment. Their quest has caused many to change denominations and even pursue other religions, cults, and sects. McIntosh says, "The church has become for them a way station or stopover on their spiritual pilgrimage."[8]

> To no surprise, then, this generation has been described today as a generation of seekers. Baby boomers have found that they have to discover for themselves what gives their life meaning, what values to live by. Unlike previous generations, boomers have decided that what really matters is a question of personal choice and experience rather than tradition. Having conquered the inner world of values, boomers increasingly added to their agenda the goal of reforming the outer world.[9]

McIntosh maintains that boomers are interested in people and not programs. They do not equate their commitment to Christ with church attendance as much as their parents did.[10] He points out:

> Perhaps because they are better educated, Boomers are sophisticated in handling money and tend to think carefully before investing it. Since they are concerned for causes and are highly relational, they want to give money to organizations that prove they are actually doing something of great value for people. They look for a return on their investment.... In the church this is seen in the desire of Boomers to support projects and people who are close to home, since it's easier to see results in local ministries.[11]

In his book *Age Wave,* Ken Dychtwald says that retirement as we know it now will soon disappear. Baby boomers will find themselves entitled to sabbaticals, time off from work with a job guarantee upon return. Some employees are allowed personal sabbaticals to pursue their own interests, while others are given community sabbaticals. Other options Dychtwald discusses are phased retirement and retirement rehearsals, part-time work and part-time retirement, flex place, and flex time. As workers move in and out of work assignments, change jobs, enter training programs, and take time off from work, volunteer mission opportunities can easily be inserted into their schedules.

Writers in both the religious and secular fields tell us that the seniors of tomorrow will continue to serve as volunteers, but they must be offered opportunities that stretch them. Many of them will respond more readily to short-term projects where they can see a finished product or event. They may be less likely to undertake long-term projects.

Helping Senior Adults Become Volunteers

Leaders of the International Mission Board and the North American Mission Board have repeatedly said that the world cannot be won by the efforts of career missionaries alone. They must have the help of volunteers. Senior adults have proven through the years that they, as volunteers, can accomplish many things for Christ.

The following questions will help senior adults determine if God wants them to be involved in volunteer missions.

1. Have you felt an unusual moving and/or stirring of God in your heart? If you are married, has your spouse had similar feelings?
2. Has God alerted you to missions/ministries you can perform?
3. Has God placed in your heart a strong desire to help others?
4. Are you available to serve, either by going away or remaining at home? Are you limited by family, heavy financial obligations, poor health, etc.?

5. Did the Lord call you previously to a special service and you were not able or did not respond to that call?

6. Has God assured you that He will provide enabling for all He may call you to do?

If the answers to several of these questions are yes, you have identified a potential missions volunteer. Look for God's leadership as you cultivate this individual. Perhaps this is God's timing to enlist him/her in volunteer missions.

Be sensitive to the needs of those you are leading. Personal conferences with senior adults who have shown interest in volunteer missions could help them work through the process of understanding God's will.

Work with your pastor and staff to create a climate for acceptance of volunteer missions in your church. Some pastors are reluctant to lose active church members or leaders, even for short-term projects. My experience has shown that senior adults who have done volunteer missions return to their churches more committed and cooperative than ever.

Pastor James Puckett of First Baptist Church in McKinney, Texas, says that volunteer missions has greatly enhanced the overall mission spirit of his church. Fifty teams from his church have participated in volunteer missions. He highly recommends volunteer missions as a great way for senior adults to minister.

Although his church members pay their own way, he says that Cooperative Program gifts in his church have increased dramatically, and each of the three special missions offerings continues to grow. Instead of decreasing his corps of volunteers for local church ministries, Puckett says the ones who go on mission trips are the first to volunteer at the church.

Actions leaders can take:
1. Explore the options that are available for volunteer missions.
2. Recruit through personal contact.

3. Ask for short-term commitments. When people have success in short-term experiences, they are more open to long-term commitments.

4. Emphasize team ministry and downplay superstar ministry.

5. Recruit on the basis of ministry and commitment to the Lord—not just on the needs of the mission field.

6. The fourth Sunday in February is Volunteers in Missions Sunday. Celebrate it in your church.

7. Every volunteer should be able to share his/her faith in a simple way. A good way to share it in a short time is the following simple outline.

   • what my life was like before I became a Christian
   • what God used to bring me to an awareness of my need of a Savior (person or circumstances)
   • what God is doing in my life today

   Churchwide witness training events and church-sponsored witnessing opportunities will help identify those who have a heart for personal evangelism.

8. Provide a house to be used as a missionary residence for furloughing missionaries. Or, provide a car for missionaries to use while on furlough. Print and distribute newsletters for missionaries.

Ask the Holy Spirit to lead in creative ways for involvement in volunteer missions. Although there are many needs calling out to senior adults for volunteering, the greatest reason to volunteer is obedience to God. The challenge remains for senior adults to ask, Lord, what will you have me do at this time in my life?

Recommended Reading:

Conspiracy of Kindness, Steve Sjogren, Servant Publications.

Ideas for Community Ministries, Joy Bolton, Women's Missionary Union, SBC.

Ideas for Nursing Home Ministries, Joy Bolton, Women's Missionary Union, SBC.

The following books are available at your Baptist Book Store or Lifeway Christian Store or you may order from Customer Service. To order, write Customer Service Center, MSN 113; 127 Ninth Avenue North; Nashville, TN 37234; call **1-800-458-2772;** fax (615) 251-5933; or email customerservice@bssb.com.

Volunteer Missions Opportunities for Senior Adults, Naomi Ruth Hunke, Women's Missionary Union, SBC, ISBN 1-5630-9105-4.

Meeting Needs, Sharing Christ, Donald A. Atkinson and Charles L. Roesel, LifeWay Press, ISBN 0-8054-9842-7.

Other Resources:

A Church's Guide to Benevolent Ministries and "How to Begin" pamphlet series, Florida Baptist Convention, Church and Community Ministries, 1230 Hendricks Avenue, Jacksonville, FL 32207, 1-904-396-2351, ext. 8251.

"How To" booklet series, Baptist General Convention of Texas, Church Ministries Department, 333 North Washington, Dallas, TX 75246-1798, 1-214-828-5389.

Church and Community Ministries and *Break Out Modules,* NAMB, SBC, 4200 North Point Parkway, Alpharetta, GA 30202-4174, 1-800-634-2462.

[1] William G. Tanner, *Hurry Before Sundown* (Nashville: Broadman Press, 1981), 25.

[2] Ibid., 67.

[3] Donald A. Atkinson and Charles L. Roesel, *Meeting Needs, Sharing Christ* (Nashville: LifeWay Press, 1995), 10.

[4] From *Conspiracy of Kindness*, © 1993 by Steve Sjogren. Published by Servant Publications, Box 8617, Ann Arbor, Michigan, 48107. Used with permission.

[5] Louis B. Hanks, *Vision, Variety, and Vitality: Teaching Today's Adult Generations* (Nashville: Convention Press, 1996), 58.

[6] Gary L. McIntosh, *Three Generations: Riding the Waves of Change in Your Church* (Grand Rapids, MI: Fleming H. Revell, 1995), 37-41, 45-51.

[7] Ibid., 55.

[8] Ibid., 97.

[9] Hanks, *Vision, Variety, and Vitality: Teaching Today's Adult Generations*, 79-80.

[10] McIntosh, *Three Generations: Riding the Waves of Change in Your Church*, 96.

[11] Ibid., 97.

Chapter 8

Recreation as a Ministry Tool

by John Garner

Recreation for a Balanced Abundant Life
Recreation as an Outreach Tool
Reaching Younger Senior Adults
Programming for Distinct Age Groups
Programming to Meet Needs
A Planning Guide
Programming Ideas
Guidelines for Planning Senior Adult Trips

Today's senior adults have more energy, better health, and longer life expectancies than previous generations. They want to use their considerable experience to contribute something worthwhile and be a part of something meaningful. Their lifestyle is a continuum of what they have been involved with earlier in life—traveling, spending, exploring, and being concerned with their quality of life.

Churches have a unique and growing opportunity to offer leisure services that can enrich the lives of senior adults. All of us have these needs.

- acceptance by others
- belonging to a group
- recognition as an individual of worth
- contribution from our life experiences
- opportunities to grow in mind, body, emotion, and spirit

These needs can be addressed through recreation ministry. This ministry tool offers a fun, relaxed way to interact with peers in a non-threatening way that is comfortable to members and non-members alike. Recreation ministry is a proven vehicle for involving and reaching prospects for the church. Churches that want to reach seniors through recreation ministry must offer quality, variety, and purpose.

Recreation for a Balanced Abundant Life

A balanced life is essential to the abundant life. Scripture tells us that "Jesus grew in wisdom and stature, and in favor with God and men" (Luke 2:52). This verse describes Jesus as a whole person with the same needs we have—to grow mentally, physically, spiritually, emotionally—throughout our lives. We do not stop growing just because we get older. In fact, we feel older when we stop taking advantage of the opportunities God gives us to grow in all these areas.

A balanced life includes recreation activities. Recreation allows God opportunity to recreate us. Breaking our routines and taking time off is essential to well-being. We are renewed and better able to handle again our work, family, and church responsibilities.

Jesus said, "I have come that they may have life, and have it to the full" (John 10:10). Recreation brings an element of joy and abundance to life. Experiencing all that life has for us redeems the time and uses it to glorify God (see Eph. 5:16-17, KJV).

Recreation as an Outreach Tool

People join groups that make them feel comfortable. Recreation offers a natural, non-threatening entry point to a senior adult group. A non-churched person may be invited by a friend to participate in an activity, such as a church aerobic class. At the event the members of the group intentionally include the non-member in conversation. The non-member gets to know the members and feels welcomed and included.

This positive experience opens the door to more involvement, perhaps in a Bible study where God's Word is shared. The Holy

Spirit takes the Word of God and gently applies it to the life of the individual. The non-member joins the Bible study group and hopefully becomes a Christian. After being a part of the group, the person grows in Christ. The new disciple begins to take on responsibilities in the church. The circle is complete when the new disciple invites another person to a church-related event.

This proven cycle of recreation as an entry point into the life of the church happens over and over across our nation. Such activities offer unique opportunities for reaching lost and unchurched seniors as well as serving a vital function in the life of the church.

Recreation activities also offer opportunities for members to help others by using their gifts, talents, and abilities learned over a lifetime. This ministry can take place as a short-term activity (on a mission project) or through a course offered at the church (as in a craft class). Not everyone is comfortable having to preach, sing, or teach; however, many are willing to share how to improve or learn a skill.

As they lead out, seniors find a recreation activity is a natural non-threatening way to share the love of Christ. The wise leader will build in opportunities for sharing Christ at meetings, outings, and on trips. Senior adults are the best at sharing with other senior adults. These sharing opportunities should not be contrived or forced. They should grow out of an overflow of genuine care and concern for the spiritual welfare of others.

Sharing the gospel must be intentional, an integral part of program planning. Otherwise, persons might as well participate in a secular outing or go to a commercially-operated gym. Church-based recreation activities should provide multiple opportunities to share one's faith.

Reaching Younger Senior Adults

Younger seniors have grown up with a leisure orientation. Before World War II, Americans were preoccupied with providing the basics (food, shelter, clothing). Since then, America has been a "land of plenty and opportunity." Americans have become increasingly affluent and leisure-oriented. Time rather than money is viewed as the valued commodity.

As America began its fundamental cultural shift after the war, the 40-hour workweek was born. Employees began to work and live for the weekend. Families began to seek out and expect quality leisure experiences. They looked for new and different places to go. As time went by, leisure became an expectation rather than a reward.

These fundamental changes in our culture have triggered the need for a new response to the expectations of seniors. This new leisure-oriented generation of senior adults—those who began turning 50 in 1996—have the time, money, and desire for recreation and fellowship. A spiritually-focused emphasis on leisure activities is a timely investment.

Gone are the days when a monthly senior adult meeting that featured a few hymns, prayer requests, a guest speaker, and a covered-dish meal would attract those entering the senior years. The expectations today are more complex. Younger seniors have differing expectations based on their experiences.

- more education
- more active lifestyles
- more varied life experiences
- financial resources
- useful work skills to share
- desire to be useful to others
- willingness to try new things
- younger self-image
- ease and convenience
- response to positive images and messages
- desire for a personal touch in services
- desire for comfortable surroundings

Programming for Distinct Age Groups

While younger and middle seniors reflect the values of the leisure generation, older seniors are cut from a different cloth. The Great Depression and World Wars I and II left their marks on how older seniors view leisure. They often do not want to be gone from home too long at a time, and they spend money cautiously. Indeed many are on fixed incomes relying heavily on Social Security.

Leisure came at a price some could not afford—so they did not plan on it in retirement. As a result, the older senior adult population finds itself unprepared to live in a leisure-oriented culture. Their thinking has been shaped by what they grew up with—primarily a strong work ethic that kept an eye on the basics of life. Nothing was certain for this age group, and nothing was taken for granted. They have a more utilitarian approach to life.

Often because of their strong work ethic, older seniors have a hard time taking advantage of their leisure. They view younger seniors as wasteful, pleasure-seeking spenders. Many have not learned to say yes to fun and recreative activity that can enrich their lives. A church's recreation ministry provides a wonderful platform to allow the whole person's growth needs to be met. In turn, seniors have the opportunity to lead a balanced, abundant life.

Church leaders will do well to note the differences in thought patterns between older and younger senior adults. A "ya'll come" general invitation to a senior adult event opens that event to all ages and mind-sets of seniors. A person 50 years of age could be involved in the same activity as a 75-year-old.

The church may need two or three groups to meet the perceived leisure needs of each senior adult. Some churches have several groups that meet at convenient times for activities that appeal to specific lifestyles. Activities and outings are tailored to meet the differing needs of the various group members.

General age-inclusive programming can work well with seniors. Persons who want to see Rome are not necessarily looking for tours made up only from their age group. However, most 50-year-olds can see Rome at a different pace from most 80-year-olds. (Notable exceptions to this rule exist!)

When all ages of seniors are represented, you must take into consideration factors such as these:

- The group may include mothers, daughters, fathers, sons.
- The group will have to move at a pace to accommodate less mobile participants.
- A clash of wills around the mind-set issues discussed earlier in this chapter often arises.
- The wider the age span the more limited the ability to target specific life needs.
- Younger and middle seniors may be less inclined to invite friends and neighbors to events that are age-inclusive.

When events are tailored to target a specific age group, either announce the age group the event is designed for or publicize physical or health requirements for participation. (An 85-year-old might want to go whitewater rafting. What stipulations would you put on such a person participating?)

Programming for younger seniors will be essential to reach a group that is reluctant to admit its own advancing age. Baby boomers turning 50 are rarely looking to identify with the senior adult ministry! Recreation will be a significant ministry tool to keep younger seniors involved and reach those who are unchurched.

Programming to Meet Needs

For any senior adult recreation ministry to succeed, good programming is a must. People are multi-dimensional. Programming in recreation must also be multi-dimensional. One size does not fit all!

Reaching people with the gospel is the ultimate goal of programming. The intangibles of fun, fellowship, relaxation, and physical fitness are added bonuses that result from this ministry.

The wise programmer will use a leadership team to help craft a purposeful and meaningful program of recreation that will capture the seniors' imaginations. The leader of the team must be a committed Christian who loves senior adults. The leader must see potential in each person, never patronizing older adults but treating them as persons of worth who have much to contribute. He or she needs to be familiar with the life changes senior adults face and how to program to meet these needs.

The leader should know the local culture, church traditions, and key lay leaders. The leader must be open to ideas that come from the team. Who better knows the needs of the group but group members themselves?

The leadership team—usually a recreation programming committee—should plan a balanced slate of activities for multiple lifestyles of seniors. The committee may be led by the church recreation minister, a lay volunteer, the church senior adult coordinator, or a church staff member. Committee members should be senior adults and senior adult leaders who represent a broad spectrum of recreational interests. They should also represent differing age groups within the senior adult age span.

The facility for senior adult meetings is not nearly as important as the programming that takes place. While a facility must be safe, clean, easily accessible, well-lighted, heated and cooled, most churches can provide these creature comforts. The key to changed lives, however, is what goes on inside and outside the building.

Programming for senior adults should have the following characteristics.

- Programming must have meaning and purpose. What is done should meet a need.
- Programming should not intentionally leave anyone out. Provide ways for all to participate, including those with disabilities, those with little discretionary money, and those with transportation problems.

- Programming should offer variety. Provide something for the goers and doers, something for the stay-at-homers, something for those who enjoy a challenge.
- Programming should be unique to the church. Adapt ideas you see, read about, or experience to your situation. No two situations are alike. Add to or take away something from another program and make it your own.
- Programming should not be repetitive. The death of the best program is doing it over and over the same way. Variety is truly the spice of life. Change the way things are done once in a while. New favorites might be discovered!
- Programming should offer plenty of time for fellowship. Seniors like to visit with their friends. Recreation programming offers a great opportunity to strengthen relationships and form new ones. The wise programmer will intentionally build "fellowship times" into the overall program.
- Programming should offer an intentional time of spiritual renewal. We are both body and soul. Do not hesitate to plan time for examining one's spiritual condition. Senior adults need opportunities to assess and grapple with spiritual issues. What better way to promote introspection than during a fall tour or on a retreat in a relaxed setting?

A Planning Guide

The following planning guide for organizing a year-long ministry can be adapted for a church of any size and for age groupings of seniors within the church. The planning process follows several steps:
1. Survey senior adults to find out their interests. Survey every three to five years. Give the survey in the largest grouping of seniors, usually Sunday School, over several weeks so that no one is left out. Also, give it to homebound and seniors who work in other areas of the Sunday School. (A sample churchwide survey is found on pp. 217-219.)

2. Tally the survey and begin by offering the most-asked-for activities first. Make sure what is offered is the very best it can be.

3. Schedule activities in conjunction with the main church calendar. All calendared activities should support the church's mission statement.

4. From the calendar of activities, develop a budget. Ask several questions when budgeting:

    a. Will the church pay for all of the expenses?

    b. Will the church ask participants to pay all the expenses?

    c. Can a combination of participant and church funds lessen the financial impact on seniors?

   Often a combination approach works best for all concerned. Lack of finances should not keep anyone from participating in some aspect of your ministry. Find ways to help seniors participate through scholarships, donations, fund-raisers, etc.

5. Promote the activities to the various groupings of seniors as creatively as possible. Be open to advertising to the community outside the church.

6. Form short-term ministry action teams—made up of several committee members or including persons outside the committee—to complete the planning and implement each event. For example, once the committee has scheduled a low-impact aerobics class, the aerobics instructor and those most interested in attending the class may form the ministry action team. Each team reports back to the committee.

7. Have participants fill out evaluation forms for the ministry as a whole as well as for individual activities. Study evaluations to know what needs to be improved, dropped, or added. These evaluations are essential for the next year's planning. The committee should be careful not to let programming simply reflect their likes and dislikes. The surveys and evaluations assure that needs are known and met.

Programming Ideas

On the next six pages you will find programming ideas in the areas of fitness/wellness, sports and games, camping, and hobbies and crafts. Within each category look for information on how to select, plan, and implement appropriate activities in your senior adult ministry. A resource list follows each idea. Use your imagination to adapt or add to these suggestions. (For other weekday programming ideas of a spiritual, educational, or ministry nature, see chap. 9.)

Fitness/Wellness

Senior adults are looking for safe, effective, and socially acceptable fitness/wellness experiences. The desire for "well living" experiences will grow as this leisure generation ages. Senior adults will be looking for certain characteristics of a fitness/wellness program.

- led by caring, competent/certified leaders
- fits their schedules
- offers information they can use at home
- helps them see results in flexibility, cardiovascular well-being, strength, and balance
- offers social interaction
- promotes spiritual growth

As you program fitness/wellness for senior adults, observe each of the following steps.

1. Pray for the right leaders. Leaders must exemplify a healthy lifestyle, both spiritually and physically, and be motivated to use fitness/wellness as a ministry tool.
2. Find the resources you will need for this ministry. Resources will include both materials and equipment. Visit ongoing programs to see what is effective. Determine the right curriculum and equipment.
3. Choose a time and place convenient for the largest number of seniors. Mornings seem to be optimal for this activity; however, senior adults who work often enjoy early evening classes. The

place needs to be large enough for uncrowded movement by the group, easy to get to, but private—a large carpeted room rather than the gym—and well ventilated, free from obstructions, and pleasantly lighted.

4. Develop a program structure that follows a basic format. One model is 3 days per week consisting of 45 minutes to an hour each day. Include warm-up, exercise, and cool-down phases. Place emphasis on stretching, range of motion, light strengthening, and balance development. Stress "doing what you can"—discourage competing with others. End each class session with a time of sharing ministry needs and prayer.

5. Adopt a pricing structure that does not prohibit anyone from participating. The most successful ministry-oriented classes are free of charge. Donations may be accepted but never solicited.

6. Advertise to the community. Local newspapers, radio, and television often offer ads for a community-based program that benefits a wide cross-section of the population. The best promotion is word of mouth from satisfied participants.

7. Round out this unique and sought-after ministry tool by following up on new class members, inviting them to Bible study and worship services. Post information about church events in dressing rooms and at the check-in counter.

Resources

Aerobirhythms Christian Music Mix, Fort Worth, TX. Comprehensive exercise plans for senior adults. Call 1-817-294-1222.

Body Recall, a program of Berea College, Berea College Press.

Nutrition for God's Temple, by Dr. Dick Couey, The Edwin Mellen Press, ISBN 0-7734-9286-0.

Exercise Programming for Older Adults, by Kay A. Van Norman, Human Kinetics Publishers, ISBN 0-8732-2657-7.

Sports and Games

Boomers have been active all their lives. They have had the opportunity to play competitive sports and to be exposed to new sports and games. Recreation programming provided by churches will need to challenge the new senior by taking him or her to uncharted waters. Innovate! Cutting edge activities will pay big dividends.

In planning sports and games, offer both skilled and unskilled activities. For example, senior adult volleyball would be considered a skilled activity whereas a board game or fishing might not require any specific skill. Adapt sports and games to fit the age group involved. A relatively new game called pickleball is adaptable for older players. Played on a badminton court, pickleball players use special wooden paddles to hit a whiffle ball across a net.

When planning sports and games for senior adults, consider the following issues.

1. The area/field needed: If you do not have adequate space, modify or drop the game.
2. The equipment needed: Can you make what you need to play the game, or is it available inexpensively?
3. Safety: Avoid activities that have been known to produce injuries in older players.
4. Participation: Can more than one or two play at a time?

The following sports activities can be used with senior adults, depending on their level of health and skill.

mixed volleyball league	hiking trips
badminton tournaments	bike trips
bowling leagues	lawn bowling
whiffle ball games	croquet
horseshoes	swimming
table games	darts/archery
shuffleboard	tennis tournaments
golf (miniature and regulation)	
newcomb (volleyball played with a ring, not a ball)	

Resource

Recreation Programming Activities for Older Adults, by Jerold E. Elliott and Judy A. Sorg-Elliott, Venture Publishing, Inc., ISBN 0-9102-5146-0.

Camping

Most senior adults love the outdoors and have participated in camping and/or fishing trips. However, the face of camping has changed vastly over the past few years. Camps are becoming more like resorts with motel-type rooms, air-conditioning, phones, and sometimes television. These adult accommodations offering all the comforts of home are finding a good reception among older adults. Campers use the facility's meeting rooms for their gathering places. Lighting and sound are good, and the climate is controlled.

When planning a camp for senior adults, consider the following:
1. What is the purpose of the event? While just getting away is worthy in itself, a larger purpose needs to be considered. Develop a theme centered around spiritual, mental, physical, and social growth. The theme needs to be supported by the agenda of the outing.
2. What type of outing will this be? A resident camp will be an experience where the "campers" stay on site over several days. At a resident camp you will have a better chance to develop a theme with continuity. You will have to consider such issues as meals, recreation, crafts, games, curriculum/study materials, accommodations, safety, staffing, and distance.

Non-resident camping opportunities can include:

Day camping—participants attend during the day and return home in the evening. Again, consider meals, safety, curriculum, recreation, facilities, staff, and distance from home.

Wilderness Camping—Primarily for physically active seniors, sleeping bags, tents, and campfires are in order here. Wilderness camping provides the opportunity to commune with God, nature, and self. Consider safety, travel, food, and preplanning. Participants need to understand the greater-than-normal physical demands. Get doctors' permissions as a precaution.

Backpacking—Often associated with wilderness camping, backpacking involves moving from point to point with a final destination in mind. Only those who are well-equipped, physically prepared, and trained should undertake this form of camping. Offer backpacking for one afternoon or as long as a week.

Travel camping—RVs are everywhere. Travel clubs attract many older adults who want to "hit the road." Although expensive, those who participate develop close friendships. Often Christian campers will be involved in a mission outing with their RVs and trailers as their home away from home.

The best camping events are short and easy to organize. They involve folks who carry part of the load of planning and running the event because they love to participate. This involvement makes many successful experiences and happy campers.

Resources
Campers on Mission, North American Mission Board, Atlanta, GA
The American Camping Association, 5000 State Rd., No. 67 North, Martinsville, IN 46151
Christian Camping International, Box 400, Somonauk, IL 60552

Hobbies and Crafts
Most of us like to create something that is either useful or attractive. Hobbies and crafts provide many programming opportunities for all ages—especially senior adults, many of whom grew up making things "from scratch." Hobbies and crafts can be a door of entrance for the unchurched or unsaved senior adult.

Hobbies and crafts can strengthen a monthly meeting, adult VBS or camping experience, or they can be offered as classes, clinics, or workshops through the recreation ministry. Leaders can usually be found among the seniors themselves. Usually, they are willing to offer their services free of charge. If sufficient interest is found in a particular area and no leader is available, offer to pay someone's way to attend a class in order for him or her to teach others.

Classes should be held in a well-lighted space large enough to accommodate participants and their supplies. Storage space is a consideration, since most hobbies and crafts will require more than one class session to complete. Not only do projects need to be stored, but supplies (paints, glues and glue guns, brushes, etc.) will need storage space as well.

Anticipate equipment that will be needed. If you project having a certain class on a regular basis, invest in purchasing the equipment. Project these costs into your recreation budget. Class fees for supplies and equipment are common; try to keep them as minimal as possible.

Consider classes in any of the following areas.

Furniture refinishing	Banner making
Basketry	Calligraphy
Ceramics	Cooking
Doll making	Flower arranging
Leather craft	Needlework
Photography	Pottery
Quilting	Smocking
Weaving	Woodworking
Seasonal crafts	Regional crafts

Resources

National Recreation and Park Association, 2775 S. Quincy St., Suite 300, Arlington, VA 22206

S&S Arts and Crafts

NASCO Arts and Crafts

Dick Blick, Inc.

Guidelines for Planning Senior Adult Trips

Trips provide many positive opportunities for senior adult involvement. Consider the following guidelines related to senior adult travel.

Types of Trips

Not all trips will interest every senior adult. Offer trips of different lengths to meet individual needs. Some seniors respond only to day trips while others keep their suitcases packed. Here are the types:

- Day Trips (points of interest within 100 miles)
- Overnight Trips (one or two nights)
- Extended Trips (a week or more)

Frequency of Trips

The frequency of trips depends on two factors: finances and scheduling. Do the senior adults finance their own trips or does the church budget supplement the cost? How will a trip affect other senior adult scheduling? A church with a well-balanced senior adult ministry has many things to schedule. Since the senior adult organization is not a "travel club," a balance must be maintained. The following is a schedule that works well:

- Day trip—every four to six weeks
- Overnight trips—two or three a year
- Extended trips—one major trip per year

Purpose of Trip

A well-planned trip has the potential of meeting needs—emotional, physical, spiritual, and social. Trips open the door to many blessings.

- New friendships are born and deeper relationships formed among the travelers.
- Seniors who have ceased traveling because they do not drive or do not want the responsibility of making travel arrangements enjoy getting out once again.

148

- Traveling with a Christian group as opposed to a secular tour interests many senior adults.
- Church trips are usually less expensive because no one is trying to make a profit.

Determining Location

1. Poll your senior adults to determine where they want to go.
2. List several options and let the group rank locations according to personal preference.
3. Plan your trip around another event, such as a senior adult Chautauqua. Plan sightseeing stops going and coming.

Options for Organizing Trips

1. Travel Agent—This option requires less effort for the senior adult coordinator. A competent travel company makes all travel arrangements, and their services are free. The senior adult coordinator sets the trip cost and collects all money. The travel agency pays bills related to their services, and the senior adult coordinator handles the rest.
2. Package Tours—Some independent bus lines and travel groups offer package trips for a set price per person. Sometimes a minimum number of travelers is required for the price quoted. The disadvantage of this option is that the company receives the profit for additional passengers beyond the minimum instead of everyone benefiting by the price reduction.
3. Self-planned Trip—Although more time consuming, if the senior adult coordinator has time and enjoys planning trips, he or she knows exactly what has been done and is in total control. The coordinator or a committee appointed to plan the trip makes all arrangements for transportation, overnight accommodations, tickets, and so on. Numerous letters and telephone calls are necessary.

Calculating Costs

1. List all estimated trip expenses.
   - transportation
   - motels and luggage handling
   - tickets
   - publicity expense, mail outs, etc.
   - meals (optional)—Will meals be included in the cost of the trip, or an additional expense?
   - sponsor's expenses
   - miscellaneous tips

2. Determine number of complimentary trips needed. The senior adult coordinator should have his/her expenses covered. Some coordinators like to invite a nurse or doctor to accompany the group on an extended trip. Cover these expenses as well.

3. Determine the minimum number of persons needed to make the trip and divide the total cost by this number.

4. Overestimate the cost of a trip rather than underestimate. Money can be refunded, but it is difficult to request more after the fee has been set. Emergencies may occur. If you realize a profit, select one of these options:
   - Refund money to the passengers.
   - Include a complimentary meal.
   - Begin a fund for future trips.
   - Discreetly offer a trip scholarship to a needy senior.

5. Prepare a medical form and require each traveler to complete it prior to the trip. In an emergency the trip coordinator must know the name and telephone number of a contact person. Special medication and allergies should be noted.

6. Provide each traveler with an itinerary at least two weeks before departure. Give names and telephone numbers where they can be reached by family.

7. Expect cancellations. Illness or an emergency cause plans to change. Try to refund as much as possible to the seniors. Occa-

sionally deposits are non-refundable after a certain date, and the trip coordinator has no way of refunding monies he cannot get back. If the senior adult club has built up a travel fund of excess moneys from pervious trips or if the trip shows a profit, make refunds.

8. Do not overload a chartered bus. Allow a seat for the drink cooler and snack box. Another empty seat is useful in case someone gets sick.

9. Limit luggage to one large suitcase and one small carry-on. Identify the group's luggage with a colored ribbon or decal.

10. Always depart on time. Be specific about where the group is to gather. Senior adults are usually very punctual, if not early.

11. Save money and time on the first day of travel by having everyone bring a sack lunch. You may furnish drinks.

12. If you anticipate a long traveling day with a late night motel stop, request that everyone pack for that one night in a small carry-on. Those needing their larger suitcase should inform the bus driver so their bags are loaded in an accessible place. Not taking all the luggage off the bus gets everyone to their rooms quicker and saves $2 to $4 per person for luggage handling.

13. On the return trip, do not give definite arrival times. Family members might wait for hours. Give approximate times and have senior adults telephone for rides at arrival.

Lodging Tips

1. Consider economical motels when all you want is a clean, comfortable bed. If the group is traveling late and plans to pull out early the next morning, eliminate luxuries.

2. Inquire about complimentary rooms. Most motels allow one free room per so many guests.

3. Note when deposits and rooming lists are required. Make a photocopy of checks mailed.

4. Request first floor rooms for senior adults.

5. Get confirmation numbers and names of contact persons.

6. Confirm all arrangements in writing and keep a copy.

7. Luggage handling is available at motels for $1–$2 per suitcase for unloading. The fee is charged again for loading the next day. If this service is desired, inform the motel prior to arrival so sufficient help is available. Passengers should have their luggage well-marked to expedite this process. Consider asking physically fit persons to serve as "bellhops" to assist others.

8. To expedite distributing room keys, request that keys be in envelopes with the occupant's names in advance of your arrival.

9. Call the motel along the road if you anticipate any delay in your arrival.

10. When arriving at a motel, leave passengers on the bus while the trip coordinator and bus driver check in.

11. Inquire about charges for local calls and long distance fees. Inform passengers and request that they not make charges to their rooms. The telephone computer in some hotels logs a long distance fee if the party does not answer in five or six rings, whether the caller is using a credit card or not. Call attention to this fee when checking out, and it may be erased.

12. Before a group disembarks from the bus, announce the next morning's departure time. Also give them the tour coordinator's room number.

13. Carry extra copies of rooming lists.

14. Keep all receipts for bills paid.

Special "Extras"

1. Carry with you juices and healthy snacks in the snack box, a large thermos of water, paper cups, paper towels, heavy plastic trash bags. Begin each day with a clean bus and clean bags.

2. As the bus leaves each morning, have Scripture reading and prayer. Use the bus microphone.

3. Prepare a "mobile library" for long trips. A large cardboard box with magazines, newspapers, crossword puzzles, and short books will help pass the time.

4. Research the areas you will be passing through and give short history lessons along the way. Members of AAA can get excellent travel guidebooks which would be helpful information sources.

5. Distribute a "daily newspaper" each morning while traveling. Duplicate these before leaving home. Include information about what you will be seeing that day, riddles and jokes, devotional thoughts, reduced map sections, trivia, and so on.

6. Prepare pencil and paper games for the bus. Accumulate small, inexpensive "gag" gifts for the winners, such as self-stick pads, decorated pencils, or refrigerator magnets.

7. Provide song sheets. Include religious and secular favorites.

8. Schedule rest stops at least every two hours. Rest areas along the highways are larger and cleaner than most restaurants. Fast food establishments can accommodate a large group without too much delay. When rest stops are combined with a meal, cafeterias are popular with seniors because of the variety and fast service.

9. Rotate seats several times a day so everyone has a chance at the front seats. Break times make convenient rotation intervals. If one side of the bus moves up while the other side moves back, passengers will visit with different people. The tour coordinator should remain in one of the front seats and eliminate it from rotation. He or she must confer with the bus driver, make announcements, lead in games, and count heads.

10. Have each side of the bus take turns getting off first. To remember which side gets off, tie a bright necktie or cloth to the metal pole in front of that side.

11. Carry a first-aid kit with bandages and ointment. Washcloths are useful. If possible, carry a wheelchair on extended trips.

12. Wear a badge identifying you as tour director.
13. At restaurants, ask to see the manager and inquire about your group eating there. Let him know you are on a tight schedule and must get in and out quickly. Ask if he compliments the tour director and bus driver.
14. Do not carry large sums of cash. Take checks already made out to motels, carry traveler's checks, or use credit cards.

Conclusion

Recreation ministries offer many opportunities to enrich and enhance the lives of senior adults. Churches that recognize the value of this ministry and offer seniors the opportunity to "recreate" will find this age group responsive. As the population of older adults increases, the demand for leisure services will increase. Churches need to be prepared for the influx of seniors wanting to take advantage of a well-planned and balanced recreation program. Churches that respond with a variety of activities will reap great benefits for participants and the church itself.

Chapter 9

Through-the-Week Ministries

by Larry Mizell

What Will Attract Younger Seniors?
Spiritual Enrichment
Learning (Growth) Opportunities
Socialization
Service Ministries

A balanced senior adult program includes what is commonly referred to as "through-the-week" ministries. Availability and interest motivate senior adults to participate in programming beyond the regular Sunday/Wednesday night activities. Retired senior adults are available during the week for a variety of activities that contribute to their spiritual, emotional, physical, and social well-being. Seniors who are still working may only work part-time or on certain days or nights.

In addition, we need to provide activities for seniors who are not available to attend Sunday activities part or all of the time because of work or family responsibilities. Increasing mobility and work-related travel may restrict Sunday attendance, as does caregiving for other family members. Seniors need flexibility in church programming just as much as other age groups.

Through-the-week activity can be defined as any activity that meets the needs of senior adults and occurs at a time other than regularly scheduled church services. These activities include senior club meetings, senior adult choir rehearsals, mission activities, trips,

155

service projects, workshops/seminars, and socials. The following four areas provide a balanced program for through-the-week activities in the local church.

- **Spiritual Enrichment**—the primary purpose of the church and the basis for all senior adult activities
- **Learning (Growth) Opportunities**—ways for seniors to expand their knowledge, understanding, and skills in all areas of life
- **Socialization**—a function of the church and a felt need on the part of senior adults
- **Service Ministries**—utilizing the talents and skills of seniors to provide for the needs of other seniors, the church family, and the community

In this chapter we will overview the variety of through-the-week activities, grouping them according to these areas. All of these activities are proven "winners" in churches across America.

Before we examine these programs, let's consider how the influx of younger seniors will impact these tried-and-true approaches to involving senior adults in through-the-week ministries.

What Will Attract Younger Seniors?

The profile of the baby boomers who began turning 50 in 1996 enables us to envision what attracts younger seniors.

Volunteerism—Younger seniors want to make their world a better place in which to live. They are eager volunteers when confronted with situations where they can make a difference. According to their lifestyles, short-term projects will have more appeal than long-term service.

Younger seniors want hands-on involvement; they want to see results. This profile indicates younger seniors will be candidates for service projects in their neighborhoods, churches, schools, communities, nation, and world. Churches must harness this vast volunteer potential to impact the world beyond their four walls.

Mentoring—Younger seniors enjoy sharing their job skills and life skills with others in one-on-one and small-group settings. Here are a few of the types of mentoring activities they can do: financial services, including budget and tax preparation, credit counseling, and household management; homemaking skills, such as cooking, sewing, gardening, home repair, and safety and security; life skills, such as conflict resolution, grief care, communication, and parenting; computer skills; and tutoring.

Churches can assign seniors to work with individuals, families, or groups in these and other areas. Encourage ingenuity and creativity. Many new and lasting friendships will result from mentoring.

Advocacy programs—Younger seniors will identify causes within the community and nation to which they will rally. Responses will include letter-writing campaigns, mailings, telephoning, staffing offices, forming advocacy groups, serving as mediators and arbitrators, and attending legislative and judicial hearings.

Churches must take seriously the concerns of younger seniors and involve them in ways that will challenge, enrich, and empower them. Through-the-week activities that are not perceived as meaningful and life-enriching will not be supported by the new crop of baby boomer seniors.

As you read the following descriptions of through-the-week ministries, consider ways they can be adapted for younger seniors.

Spiritual Enrichment

Every church-sponsored activity should have a spiritual component. Otherwise this question can be raised, Why is this activity church-based? In chapter 3, several ideas were included for through-the-week Bible studies. (Refer to pp. 48-50 for information on weekday Bible studies, adult Vacation Bible Schools, homebound ministry, conference call Sunday School classes, read-the-Bible through emphases, and Bible conferences.) Other weekday Bible-based events include senior adult retreats, senior adult revivals, and senior-led prayer groups. A model for each of these is given below. Adapt the model for your church, keeping in mind the ages and lifestyle issues of your seniors.

Senior Adult Retreat

A get-away from the hustle and bustle of the world inspires and motivates seniors. They like a streamlined schedule with built-in fellowship. The length of a retreat can vary from one day to five days.

- **One-Day Retreat**–appealing because it does not require lodging and is less expensive. Choose a nearby location to allow time for the program.
- **Overnight Retreat**–provides more time for study and participation. This site could be farther from the church.
- **Five-Day Retreat**–allows for more spiritual enrichment, recreation, and free time. Travel time can be from four to six hours one way.

Appoint a steering committee three to six months in advance to select the location, establish the cost, and choose a theme. With date and location decided, subcommittees can begin their work.

- **Program**–Select program personnel and plan activities which interpret the theme and accomplish the purpose.
- **Arrangement**–Coordinate conference rooms and special equipment (audio, video, overhead projectors, etc.) needed by program leaders.
- **Registration**–Determine the best way to register the participants and the payment schedule. Pre-registration might be handled by the church office. At the retreat site provide name tags, programs, and room assignments.
- **Publicity**–Plan creative publicity for mail outs, posters, and announcements for Sunday School classes, newsletters, and worship services.
- **Transportation**–Decide on the mode of transportation to the retreat site and make arrangements. Transportation on a

bus, mini-bus, or van is more fun and safer than a caravan of individual cars.

- **Food**—Make decisions concerning meals and snacks. At a camp or motel/resort, menu choices and cost must be discussed with the food service director. Keep in mind the special dietary needs of many seniors. If you provide food, the committee should arrange for the cook, plan the menu, and purchase the food and snacks.
- **Recreation**—Organize recreation and free time. Schedules would include early morning exercises, afternoon hikes and walking, crafts, sightseeing, and fellowships. Table games are popular. Prizes, ribbons, or trophies add excitement.

Here are some typical schedules for the three types of retreats:

ONE-DAY RETREAT

Depart church—8:00 a.m.
Welcome/light refreshments—8:45 a.m.
Bible study—9:00 a.m.
Break—9:45 a.m.
Worship/music and speaker—10:15 a.m.
Lunch—11:15 a.m.
Rest, relaxation, games—12:15 p.m.
Closing/inspirational—2:00 p.m.
Refreshments/depart for home—3:00 p.m.

OVERNIGHT RETREAT

Depart church for retreat site after lunch
Registration—4:00 p.m.
Dinner—5:00 p.m.
Session 1—6:30 p.m.
Break—7:30 p.m.
Entertainment, snacks—7:45 p.m.
Good night—8:45 p.m.
The Next Day:
Exercise—6:30 a.m.

Breakfast—7:00 a.m.

Quiet time—8:00 a.m.

Bible study—8:45 a.m.

Break—9:30 a.m.

Personal interest conferences—9:45 a.m.

Worship/music and speaker—10:45 a.m.

Lunch—11:45 a.m.

Recreational time, table games, rest—12:45 p.m.

Personal interest conferences—2:00 p.m.

Depart for home—3:00 p.m.

FIVE-DAY RETREAT

Use the above schedule, adding afternoon options:

- trips to interesting sites in the area
- recreational tournaments
- table games
- exhibits
- arts and crafts

Dinner—5:00 p.m.

Entertainment/fellowship/talent show or

Worship/music—6:45 p.m.

Good night—8:45 p.m.

Senior Adult Revival

A churchwide revival is planned and implemented by senior adults, usually with a senior adult-aged revival team of preacher and music leader. Today's seniors enjoy a revival reminiscent of the 1950s, with gospel music and heart-warming, soul-stirring messages.

Services are held during the day with the possible exception of Sunday and Wednesday nights. A Sunday morning through Wednesday night schedule is popular. Here are 10 essential steps in preparation.

1. Set a date on the church calendar convenient for seniors. Avoid winter months.

2. Enlist the preacher and musicians well in advance.

3. Decide on days of the week and time. The day schedule should begin at mid-morning and end with lunch. The revival service should be no longer than one and a half hours.

4. Have your senior adult choir sing with special music by senior adults themselves. Consider asking senior adult choirs from area churches to be the featured choir at different services.

5. Set up prayer groups and have home prayer meetings the week preceding the revival.

6. Enlist and train counselors for invitation counseling.

7. Plan potluck meals or provide meals for a small fee.

8. Enlist senior adult ushers and greeters to provide warm welcomes.

9. Use your Sunday School for follow-up to visitors.

10. Design publicity with seniors in mind—large print, easy-to-read, to the point, and clear in direction and times. Many communities have senior adult papers. Utilize these to get to your target audience. Use free media.

Senior Adult Prayer Groups

Prayer can be offered any place, anytime by anyone. Prayer is not dependent on health, mobility, resources, or age. No physical exam is required! As a result, prayer is an activity especially relevant to senior adult ministries.

Seniors are experienced and motivated prayer warriors. Many of them say they finally have the time for prayer they have been looking for all of their lives! *Church Prayer Ministry Manual* by T.W. Hunt (ISBN 0-7673-1908-7) provides detailed information on how to begin a prayer ministry in your church and is available from Customer Service (1-800-458-2772).

Like any other spiritual discipline, the prayer habit must be cultivated. Here are several ways to make our prayer efforts more intentional.

Weekday prayer groups—Groups can meet in homes or at the church. Prayer concerns can be provided to groups by Sunday School classes, the church office, and the International and North American Mission Boards. Members should be encouraged to maintain an updated prayer list. Ensure that the group prays, rather than meeting to talk about prayer concerns.

Prayer chains—Members of prayer chains generally keep in contact by telephone. Prayer concerns are given to chain members by other church members and the church office. Each person on the chain is linked to the others, so that no matter who gets the first call, the prayer concern is shared with everyone on the chain.

Prayer walks—Persons walk through a neighborhood and pray for individuals and families in the residences and businesses as they pass. This ministry gives recreational walkers new purpose and meaning to their regular morning or afternoon walks. For more information on prayer walking, contact Randy Sprinkle at the International Mission Board at 1-804-219-,208.

Prayer line—Seniors can answer calls received on a church-sponsored prayer line publicized to the community.

Prayer room—Some churches set aside a room in their building for 24-hour-a-day prayer. Some of these ministries allow seniors to pray in their homes, rather than coming to the church.

Learning (Growth) Opportunities

The concept of lifelong learning does not have to be preached to younger seniors. Technological advances and the fast-paced changes of the past 50 years have made it impossible to rest on the laurels of what we once knew! In the future, continuing education will be essential, not optional.

Churches that want to attract unchurched and unsaved seniors should make their facilities available for short-term classes on a variety of subjects. Several models and descriptions of educational programs are given to spur your thinking.

Seminars/Workshops

Schedule these sessions over lunch or in the evening to encourage adults who are still employed to attend. Here are a few interesting seminar topics:

Confronting losses

Achieving wholeness

Biblical issues of aging

Living alone

Retirement planning

Volunteer opportunities

Home maintenance
and repair

Estate/will planning

Building relationships
between generations

Consumer fraud/
safety and security

Adjusting to retirement

Housing options

Adapting to change

Caregiving for the elderly

Defensive driving

Living on fixed income

Social Security (Medicare,
Medicaid, food stamps, etc.)

Car maintenance and repair

Governmental programs
for senior adults

Role reversal for spouses and/
or grown children/parents

Interest Groups

Interest groups attract persons with the same hobbies, talents, and abilities. Classes can be ongoing or short-term. Groups may meet weekly or monthly. Teachers or facilitators who lead the groups are volunteers who share a similar passion for the subject. Members of the group pay for all supplies.

Some of the many types of interest groups include cooking classes for men who have lost their wives, gardening and lawn care, piano, handbells, aerobics, ceramics, bird-watching, journal-writing, genealogy, library skills, simple mechanics, photography, basic electronics, fitness, nutrition, painting, calligraphy, foreign language, writing, current events, computers, needlework, and quilting. (Refer to pp. 146-147 for information on hobby/craft groups and how to incorporate them into a church recreation ministry.)

Back-to-School Emphasis

Plan a "Back-to-School" emphasis in the fall to last one day or extend for several mornings. Utilize qualified, volunteer persons to teach in their areas of expertise. Preregister participants for classes.

Classes are repeated, with up to three classes each day. Provide table games and crafts daily for those with free time between classes. See the list of possible topics for classes under the headings of Seminars/Workshops and Interest Groups on the previous page.

Here is a sample schedule for a five-day school:

Monday
9:30 a.m.–Opening Session (prayer, introductions, orientation)
10:00–10:50 a.m.–First class
11:00–11:50 a.m.–Second class
Noon–Lunch–Sack lunch, potluck, chili, or hamburgers
12:30–1:20 p.m.–Third class
Tuesday-Thursday–Classes begin at 10:00 and follow the same schedule as Monday.
Friday–Educational field trip

Community Adventures in Learning

Join with churches in your city to offer educational opportunities. Form a "Community Adventures in Learning Council" to initiate and organize the program. Each church should have equal representation. Elect a chairperson, vice-chairperson, secretary, and treasurer. Ask volunteer, retired seniors to teach other senior adults.

Determine the most appropriate location to meet. A large activity area is needed with classrooms nearby. Several churches may have adequate facilities and wish to host the program. If so, maintain the same location until the end of a series of studies. Then rotate to another church for the next series of studies.

Invite community groups such as hospitals, nursing services, and civic clubs to "affiliate" with the program to lend their approval and support. Ask "affiliate" staff members to teach classes.

Select a day and time to meet each week. A suggested time from 10:00 a.m. to noon allows for coffee, fellowship, announcements, and class time. Follow with lunch, if possible.

Sessions are six weeks and may be scheduled four times a year–winter, spring, summer, and fall. Allow a break between sessions.

Survey seniors in each sponsoring church to discover possible teachers. Prepare attractive publicity with detailed descriptions of classes, dates, times, and teachers. List "affiliates" and sponsoring churches. Attach a registration form.

A nominal registration fee might be charged to cover miscellaneous expenses for the program. Each sponsoring church could be asked to contribute to the operating budget.

Intergenerational Activities

Offer a weekend workshop for all ages where "families," made up of different age groups and not related to each other, complete a series of activities designed to get them to work together to accomplish a goal. The purpose is to allow senior adults to interact with and mentor younger members of the congregation.

Resources

Church Family Gatherings: Programs and Plans, by Joe H. Leonard, Jr., Books on Demand, ISBN 0-608-00217-8.

Intergenerational Religious Education, by James W. White, Religious Education Press, ISBN 0-8913-5067-5.

National and State Conferences

The Adult Discipleship and Family Development Department, Life-Way Christian Resources, offers numerous enrichment events each year. For detailed information, write: Senior Adult Events, MSN 151, 127 Ninth Ave. N., Nashville, TN 37234. In addition, your state Baptist convention offers events and training. Many seniors enjoy attending their annual state evangelism conference.

Senior Adult Chautauquas—Held each fall in various locations around the country, these senior adult week-long gatherings include Bible studies, worship, seminars, fellowship, and sightseeing.

Senior Adult Spring Flings—Spring events across the country with a convention format, they feature nationally-known speakers and singers.

Senior Adult Christmas Celebration—This annual event is a holiday celebration at Ridgecrest Conference Center in North Carolina. Christmas attractions in the area, such as the Candlelight Evening Biltmore tour, add to the festive, joyful worship experiences.

Support Groups

Some churches have ongoing support groups for widows and widowers. Other groups offer support in dealing with aging parents, health issues, family relationships, stroke victims, and Alzheimer's.

LIFE Support Group Series Training Video (ISBN 0-8054-9881-8) available from Customer Service (1-800-458-2772) provides resources for leaders/members of groups. *WiseCounsel: Skills for Lay Counselors* (ISBN 0-7673-2615-6) is a resource to train facilitators, or contact your association or state Baptist convention for training.

Life Review Workshop

Conduct life review workshops to help seniors gain a fuller understanding of who they are. Continuing to grow in old age requires coming to terms with the past yet not becoming lost in it. Life review is designed to lead persons in experiencing their life events holistically.

Oral History Group

Recalling memories of former years is not only therapeutic to the person but valuable as oral history. Cassette recorders and video cameras make oral history projects simple and fun. Train senior adults in interviewing techniques and the use of a video camera.

Oral history also involves youth, young adults, median adults, and senior adults in an intergenerational activity.

Resources:

Oral History for Texans, by Thomas L. Charlton, Texas Historical Commission, P.O. Box 12276, Austin, Texas 78711 (1985). Information on interviewing and recording techniques.

Check in professional journals for articles such as these below:

E. M. Donahue, "Preserving History Through Oral History Reflections," *Journal of Gerontological Nursing,* 8.5 (1982): 272-278.

K. Huber and P. Miller, "Reminisce with the Elderly—Do It!," *Geriatric Nursing,* 5.2 (1984): 84-87.

Reading Programs

Seniors have the opportunity to enjoy leisure reading. Take advantage of that interest by forming groups for book reviews. Secure a good storyteller and a book that would appeal to senior adults. Have the book available to buy or check out from your church or local library.

Check with your local Christian bookstore for authors that will be coming to your area and secure them to give programs on their books. Other ways to encourage reading good literature include:

Life Enrichment Diploma for Senior Adults—The Christian Growth Study Plan requires the study of six books to receive the Life Enrichment Diploma. These books can be studied individually or taught in your senior adult clubs. For diploma details write: Senior Adult Section, Family Ministry Department, MSN 151, 127 Ninth Avenue, North, Nashville, Tennessee 37234.

Certificate Program—Design your own reading program with the assistance of your church librarian. Present a certificate to those completing the program.

Lending library—Encourage seniors to lend books to each other. Contribute "fines" for overdue books to a mission project.

Bookmobile—If your community has a bookmobile, find out where it stops and publicize this information to your seniors. A mobile cart filled with books from your church library can be your church's bookmobile, circulating during senior adult functions.

Talking books—Seniors can record books on tape or can secure these and distribute them to homebound, nursing homes, and senior residential communities. Many who can no longer read would appreciate having the church newsletter or other churchwide communications on tape.

Continuing Education Programs

Community colleges offer a wide variety of learning opportunities through continuing education departments. Some colleges give free tuition to those 65 or older. Check on Artists and Lecture Series. They are usually free or at discount rates to senior adults.

Areas of study for continuing education might include computer basics, the Internet, sign language, foreign languages, estate planning/taxes, self-defense, or First Aid/CPR.

Some colleges, including Baptist colleges and universities, offer summer institutes for seniors. Encourage retirees to consider Elderhostel programs. For more information write: Elderhostel, 80 Boylston, Suite 400, Boston, Massachusetts, 02116.

Field Trips

Trips can be educational as well as entertaining. Some of these learning opportunities include theaters; fairs; local industries; radio and television stations; zoos; wildflower or autumn leaf trips; airports; denominational retirement centers, schools, or headquarters; mission centers; old cemeteries; historic homes; and museums.

Film Festival

Many free films are available from public libraries, extension departments, and businesses. Video stores have sections of older movies that provide an evening of nostalgia. Set up a fellowship area like a movie theater, complete with refreshments. Rent a popcorn machine for the evening. Enlist ushers and print tickets. Free films can be obtained from these sources:

University of North Texas, Center for Studies in Aging. Request catalogue from Gerontological Film Collection, Media Library, P.O. Box 12898, University of North Texas, Denton, Texas 76203.

Modern Talking Picture Service: Outstanding free-loan 16mm films/videocassettes for adult groups. Their address is: Modern Talking Picture Service, 5000 Park Street, North, St. Petersburg, Florida 33709-9989.

Socialization

Church is a family of faith. Friendships made at church are often the most meaningful relationships in a senior adult's life, especially when immediate family lives far away. Provide opportunities for seniors to befriend each other—the biblical principle of *koinonia* (see 1 John 1:7).

Recognitions

Special days in the life of the church should be set aside to recognize senior adults for their accomplishments and faithfulness. Here are a few types of recognition services.

Oscar Awards—Have a banquet during which every senior present receives an award for an outstanding personal trait, spiritual quality, or accomplishment. Follow these steps to prepare.
1. Make a list of every senior adult member who will attend. Determine the most outstanding characteristic of each person. Try not to duplicate.
2. Prepare awards—ribbons or certificates—organized by categories such as spiritual gifts, talents, accomplishments, or character traits. Put awards into envelopes labeled with each category.

3. Select people to present the Oscars by categories, but be sure they will not call their own names.

4. Have either potluck or a catered meal. Decorate tables with a black and white color theme, using an accent color like red.

5. Prepare posters that use the theme colors and place these in all Sunday School departments of senior adults. Send out invitations. Emphasize that everyone is to receive an award.

6. Print a program that uses the theme colors and list all of the categories that will be awarded. Leave a blank beside each award so seniors can fill in the name when the award is given.

After dinner and special music have your pastor or senior adult leader give a short talk about the importance of every individual to God. Have presenters call out the categories, open the envelopes, and award the certificates. Let everyone come to the platform and receive his or her award (do not rush the participants). Give each person equal time and recognition. Close with prayer thanking God for the gifts He has given each person.

Family Dinner and Talent Show—This activity allows senior adults to share their family's talents with everyone. Have the program at night so that families can come. Encourage seniors to bring all their family members, whether or not they perform. Arrange the program for variety, interchanging singing, playing an instrument, reading a poem, etc. Arrange to have a stage, sound system, and piano.

50th Wedding Celebration—Honor couples who have celebrated 50 years or more of marriage.
Preparation:
1. Determine the couples that qualify.
2. Print invitations to be sent to all church members and others designated by the honorees.
3. Decorate with flowers, greenery, and candles.
4. Provide cake and punch for a reception after the ceremony.

5. Enlist a wedding director to plan the ceremony and conduct the rehearsal.
6. Publicize the ceremony in your church and community.
7. Hold a rehearsal dinner. (Optional)

Ceremony:

1. Use grandchildren of honorees as ushers and candlelighters.
2. Have ushers seat all guests.
3. Each couple will slowly walk down the aisle. Have a long-stemmed flower for each lady and a boutonniere for each man.
4. Have honorees take a seat on the platform or stand along the front of the room.
5. Have the pastor conduct the ceremony, introduce each couple, give their year of marriage, and ask family and friends to stand.
6. Dismiss with prayer. Invite everyone to the reception.

Homebound Day—Recognize homebound members, their families, and homebound workers with a special day of appreciation. Acknowledge homebound workers and caregivers during a morning worship service. If your church is televised, include the homebound in the observance of the Lord's Supper via television. Assign deacons to deliver the bread and juice to the homes of those wishing to participate.

Senior Adult Day—The first Sunday in May is designated Senior Adult Day on the Southern Baptist Convention calendar. However, select a date appropriate for your church. Senior Adult Day is a good way to begin Christian Home Emphasis, the first week of May on the Southern Baptist Convention calendar.

Preparation:

Select a Senior Adult Day Planning Committee. You may use the senior adult council or a special planning committee. This committee secures the date, determines the schedule and activities for the day, and appoints sub-committees.

- **Attendance**—Make it high attendance in the Senior Adult Sunday School. Set goals; recognize those who reach goals.
- **Worship Service**—Invite a guest speaker or ask your own pastor to preach on the selected theme. Use seniors for special music, ushering, Scripture reading, and testimonies.
- **Ministry**—Select one or more ministry activities to be done during the day or week.
- **Fellowship**—Have a luncheon following the morning worship service or have a Sunday night after-church fellowship. When a Sunday fellowship is not practical, try a Saturday night banquet or a Saturday afternoon outing.
- **Transportation**—Provide transportation to senior adults who cannot attend regularly or need transportation.
- **Publicity**—Publicize activities well in advance of the event.

Area Rally

Plan an old-fashioned day of fun, food, and fellowship. Invite seniors from several churches in the area. Here is an agenda:
10:00—Get acquainted time—name tags, coffee, and snacks
10:30—11:25—First Rally Session (speaker, choirs, special music, entertainment)
11:30—12:00—Recreation, games, contests between the churches
12:00—12:45—Lunch (catered, covered dish, or sack lunch)
1:00—2:00—Second Rally Session

Fall Enlistment Dinner

When summer ends and school begins, gather seniors for a fun dinner. Select an appropriate theme and decorate accordingly. Create a restaurant atmosphere by having individual tables of six to eight instead of tables lined end to end. Enlist a host and hostess for each. Make this an outreach event, inviting senior adult prospects to be your guests.

Fall Festival

Decorate a large room with fall colors. Plan booths such as sponge-throws, fishing, cakewalk, ringtoss, bowling, and balloon darts. A dunking booth with the pastor and staff as victims guarantees a crowd. Admission to the party is a sack of candy, which becomes treats and prizes throughout the evening.

Parties

Birthday Parties—Include all senior adults or just those having birthdays that month. If the party is only for the birthday celebrities, allow them to bring a guest. Always invite the pastor and staff to celebrate the occasion. For a yearly birthday celebration, designate a table for each month of the year, and ask seniors to sit with others born in the same month. Tables are cleverly decorated to reflect the emphasis of that month. Have a sing-a-long with an appropriate song for each month.

Funny Face Party—Let the senior adults sponsor a "Funny Face" party and involve the entire church in some intergenerational fun. Decorate the fellowship hall or a large room with a party theme. Have several face painters to custom-design faces or let participants paint their own faces. Give prizes for categories.

Christmas party for foster children in the community or for special education students. The Department of Human Services and the school administration office can provide names and addresses. If planned in advance, the entire church can become involved through contributions, committees, and transportation of children.

Here are some resources for party ideas:

Party Mix: 21 Creative Plans for Fun Fellowship, by Karol Ladd, Broadman and Holman Publishers, ISBN 0-8054-6095-0.

Recreation Programming Activities for Older Adults, by Jerold E. Elliott and Juday A. Sorg Elliott, Venture Publishing, Inc., ISBN 0-9102-5146-0.

Senior Center

Some churches own homes near the church building that can be converted to a senior center. Centers are staffed by seniors and are open during the day and for special events. Classes can be held there, and seniors can gather for table games and fellowship as well.

Drama Groups

Drama groups may perform their own drama writings or those of others, including storytelling, pantomime, tableau, pageantry, and choral speaking. Drama groups can sponsor talent shows or fashion shows as all-church fellowships. A puppet ministry can involve seniors in outreach events at parks, recreation areas, and malls. Include puppets at VBS also.

Dinner Clubs

Dinner clubs meet in members' homes on a rotating basis or at a different restaurant each month or once a quarter. Sometimes known as "Knife and Fork Clubs," they attract persons who like to eat out together. Choose the site for each get together and make reservations for the number who will attend. Use it as a witnessing tool to attract unsaved and unchurched seniors.

Service Ministries

These services can be implemented by seniors. (For services provided to seniors, refer to pp. 86-90.) Begin by surveying seniors to determine the volunteer opportunities that interest them, their skills and abilities, and services they might need. A sample survey is found on pages 217-219.

"Senior Hands" Projects

Picture a group of seniors scraping and painting a house for a needy family, rebuilding a porch, developing a park, or cleaning up a neighborhood. Select a major project that can be accomplished in four to five work days, and let the senior adults lead in this community service.

Housing Ministry
Consider adopting a multi-family housing complex or building. Senior adults can offer Bible studies, children's programs, recreation, or arts and crafts. Talk with the manager of the facility to determine possibilities. Invite residents to events at the church and if necessary provide transportation to and from the event.

Beautify the Church
Senior adults assume responsibility for improving the church landscape or doing minor remodeling inside. Seniors can have a special ministry by tackling the small, neglected tasks. Spring cleaning is always appreciated. This ministry can be on-going or seasonal.

International Neighbors
International students attending college in the United States enjoy visiting in American homes. Several adults may join together to periodically entertain the students. Or, individual seniors may "adopt" an international student for a year or more. Occasionally, there is need for housing when dormitories close for the holidays.

School Helpers
Retired adults find meaningful service in assisting public schools. Some pupils need private tutoring in basic scholastic skills. Visit with the school principal to discover possibilities for this ministry. One church combined tutoring with table games and recreation to provide incentive for children to attend the after-school program.

Community Advocates
Senior adults interested in public affairs can be advocates for worthwhile causes. An organized telephone/letter writing committee can

influence local and state government officials. Issues such as child abuse, benefits for the elderly, gambling, or local decisions need strong Christian voices. (See p. 157 for other advocacy options.)

Senior Sitters

Seniors can provide baby-sitting for young adults in the church to assist them in their ministry activities. Or, seniors can offer to stay in homes of people who are attending funerals. Form a group who will sit with people in hospitals or who will sit with families during surgery of family members.

Card Ministry

Those who are limited in physical abilities can still minister through cards. Sending birthday cards to seniors or other church members always encourages the recipient. A significant ministry is sending sympathy cards and words of encouragement to persons who have lost loved ones.

Mentoring Services

Seniors have job skills and life skills that can enrich the lives of others. Here are some ways seniors can mentor: Help young adults with family budget planning. Teach persons how to plan and cook budget meals. Teach young people how to sew and mend clothes. Help immigrants with shopping and other informational services. Advise senior adults who desire assistance in major decisions regarding housing alternatives, finances, and legal matters. Help persons fill out forms such as tax reports, insurance and medical claims, and Social Security. Compile a list of volunteers who will respond when other seniors need help.

Jail/Prison Ministry

Seniors are discovering the rewarding ministry of working with prisoners, victims, and family members. Volunteers are needed for mentoring inmates, tutoring, and teaching Bible study and discipleship classes. For information, obtain a copy of *The Criminal Justice Ministry Manual: Producing Shalom* (ISBN 0-7673-9114-4).

Holiday Helpers

Primarily a Christmas group, Holiday Helpers repair and distribute toys, Christmas shop for homebound, take groups of needy children shopping, baby-sit for single parents so they can shop without their children, and prepare and deliver holiday decorations to children's hospitals, nursing, and retirement homes.

Disaster Relief

Seniors collect, repair, and distribute clothing, furniture, and other items for disaster relief centers. Many state conventions have a disaster relief unit that you can work with. These units go to disaster areas and remain there until the immediate crisis has passed.

Hospital Equipment

Establish a check-out service for equipment—hospital beds, wheelchairs, walking canes, commode chairs, and other items persons need in order to remain in their own homes while recuperating.

Home Security Committee

Organize a volunteer committee to inspect homes of seniors for safety. Provide a request form to be signed by individuals wishing consultation. Provide a program on prevention techniques and personal safety. Purchase an engraving tool and assist seniors in marking home valuables. The local police and fire departments are good resources for this program.

Chapter 10

Financial Planning for Senior Adults

by J. David Carter

Teach Responsibility to Care for Older Members
Help Your Church Members Choose Advisors
Prepare Seniors for Retirement
Encourage Financial Preparations for Death
Consider Volunteerism As Stewardship
Plan Your Church's Response

A comprehensive senior adult ministry will include financial planning. Providing integrity-based financial planning assists members presently living on fixed incomes, while preparing younger seniors for retirement. In addition, your church will benefit from knowing how to encourage persons who do not have a habit of charitable giving. Younger results-oriented seniors need information about creative giving approaches which challenge their desire to make a difference in their world. Older seniors respond to how their money can bless the church and others even after death.

Often a neglected area of ministry, financial planning makes a statement about a person's stewardship of life. Most financial emphasis in churches focuses on the budget, mission giving, and buildings. Church members get little help in making spiritually-sound financial decisions, although many of them turn first to persons in their churches when they have major financial issues.

Financial planning includes estate planning, wills, trusts, transfer of wealth, taxes, how to access private information after a death, investment risks, Social Security, retirement income plans, and safe investing.

Teach Responsibility to Care for Older Members

One of the responsibilities of the church is instruction on the biblical mandate to care for the elderly among us. The early apostles were confronted with the need to minister to widows. Out of that concern, the office of deacon was established (see Acts 6:1-7).

The church can begin by helping families anticipate the needs of their older members. My father lived to be 80 years of age and my mother is still living. One of my brothers and his wife sacrificed to care for them at home, but their needs were too great. We had to move them to a nursing home. My mother is still there. My wife and I joyfully help with the finances.

Years earlier we had anticipated my parents' needs. When the money was needed to pay for dad's funeral expenses, it was already there. Families must plan for the possibility of long-term care and/or funeral expenses.

Paul said, "If anyone does not provide for his relatives, and especially for his immediate family, he has denied the faith and is worse than an unbeliever" (1 Tim. 5:8). If believers live by what God teaches, "[He] will meet all your needs according to his glorious riches in Christ Jesus" (Phil. 4:19). His "riches in Christ Jesus" are more than sufficient! We must exercise wisdom in money matters. Much of this wisdom comes from knowing how to seek advice.

> Blessed is the man who finds wisdom, the man who gains understanding, for she is more profitable than silver and yields better returns than gold. She is more precious than rubies; nothing you desire can compare with her. Long life is in her right hand; in her left hand are riches and honor (Prov. 3:13-16).

In financial planning, as in all areas of life, a wise person seeks counsel from God's Word.

> Blessed is the man who does not walk in the counsel of the wicked or stand in the way of sinners or sit in the seat of mockers. But his delight is in the law of the Lord, and on his law he meditates day and night. He is like a tree planted by streams of water, which yields its fruit in season and whose leaf does not wither. Whatever he does prospers (Ps. 1:1-3).

When I pastored in Florida, I saw many retirees grow older lacking sufficient income to sustain them without food stamps and Medicaid. By necessity, I became proficient at helping them obtain some of those resources. Although they did not want to take governmental aid, their survival literally depended on it. During that time, I led the churches to offer estate planning conferences.

What can you do to help your members prepare for retirement and aging? What can you do to help families care responsibly for their own? One approach is to help them find competent advisors.

Help Your Church Members Choose Advisors

Christian professionals are in business to make a living. If such persons have a product or service to sell, they will not be completely unbiased when asked for advice. This fact does not make them unscrupulous. It just means they are not totally motivated by altruism.

We routinely hear of shams designed to get money from well-intentioned Christians. Before referring a church member for professional advice, compile a list of capable, honest professionals in your community. Professional planners or advisors can be grouped in three general categories.

Commission-based planners make their money by charging a commission for their services. Whether this is good or bad has to do with the integrity of the planner. If he sells a mutual fund, he gets a "load" which is a percentage charge paid by the mutual fund company. At other times, the commission is paid by the investor. This type of financial planner can be motivated by the mutual fund company more than by the investor. In many cases, the planner represents the company, and not the Christian coming to him for help. His motivation has the potential to be more self-focused.

Brokers earn money by handling transactions for their clients. They make money based on the dollar and quantity volume of the sales. Most are honorable persons of integrity, but beware. Just because they have a nice paneled walnut office in a large bank building does not mean that they have your church member's interest at heart. A friend of mine recently settled a lawsuit with a major company because his broker mishandled his account. My friend had signed a power-of-attorney giving the broker the right to manage his funds. The broker created commissions for himself by buying and selling stocks (churning) until my friend lost a great deal of money. He won the lawsuit and recovered part of his money. Obviously, there are good and bad professionals in every business.

Fee-only advisors will serve you without representing any company or selling you anything. Some financial counselors use the term "fee-based," which means they make a fee based on what they sell. A genuine fee-based financial counselor's only source of income is the charge for the time spent with a client; in other words, this counselor will charge by the hour. He builds a client list by being successful in giving good advice. The good advice given to one person, however, may not apply to another. This professional needs to be capable of discovering the individual needs, goals, and risk tolerance levels of each individual client.

Sources for Discovering the Right Professional

1. Ask a reputable Christian banker to give you a name. Many banks have persons who fit in one or more of the categories

listed above. Get references from several bankers. Remember, each will likely recommend someone from his own bank first.

2. Ask a Christian Certified Public Accountant (CPA). Some CPAs also give financial management advice, but most will refer you to someone else, or no one at all. They are somewhat liable for their advice, be it good or bad, so they will hesitate to give a good recommendation for anyone.

3. Ask a trusted attorney. Attorneys handle all sizes of estates and will know persons in the investment fields. Your church members need an attorney to prepare wills and other documents. Attorneys are becoming more specialized. All attorneys are not good at financial planning. Be sure to check the credentials of the attorney. Even well-meaning professionals have limitations.

4. Ask several church members who they use. Satisfied customers are often a credible referral source.

5. Check to see if the advisor is registered, and whether he or she has a track record of problems, by calling the Securities Exchange Commission at 1-800-732-0030 (or write them at 450 Fifth St. NW, Washington, DC 20549).

6. Some churches have directories that provide a list of professionals who are church members. If you have not compiled your own, ask churches in your area for such a list.

7. Call a local college or university that has a finance department. Ask professors educated in finance or banking. They may have a list of qualified professionals or may give further advice on how to choose one.

8. Another great source is the Baptist Foundation in your state. Contact your state convention office. They have credible persons on staff to direct you to the right decision.

Prepare Seniors for Retirement

"[Seniors] will need about 70 to 90 percent of [their] pre-retirement income to live comfortably during retirement."[1] "Only 26 percent [of Americans] believe they are socking away the correct amount. Seventy-three percent admitted they are saving too little. Indeed, only 40 percent said they have a savings plan, although on average, workers said they plan to retire at age 62."[2]

Significant Differences Between Adult Age Groups

Nancy Ammerman, Don Chase, and Charles Montgomery studied the characteristics of various types of stewards in churches today. The characteristics and guidelines enumerated below may not apply to all churches alike but can be helpful in designing an approach to financial planning.[3]

1. **Strivers**—born before 1931. They dislike debt both for themselves and for their church. They were taught stewardship in how to give, where to give, and what portion to give. They believe it is important to meet a budget.

2. **Challengers**—born between 1932 and 1945. They were primarily influenced by postwar prosperity in America. They have seen the structure of home life depreciate, contributing to numerous problems. Stewardship was not a clear message from their homes. Values became unclear during the 1960s. They are utilitarian in their choices—does it work for me? There is almost no agreement on what is right for everyone.

3. **Calculators (baby boomers)**—born between 1946 and 1964. They grew up with a high tech, rapidly changing, mobile society. They are accustomed to using a computer manual to run machines and want a manual to run the church. They do not often see the Bible as that manual, but they can be taught and are thrilled when they learn. The biblical teaching of stewardship is not an ingrained part of their lives. Many boomers view the Cooperative Program as impersonal, and boomers want to become personally involved. They expect to receive a return on their giving. They are bottom-line folks.

A Transfer of Wealth

By the year 2010, boomers will inherit as much as $11 trillion. They will suddenly have access to a lot of money. Many consider this money their birthright, having paid for their parents' lifestyle through Social Security paycheck deductions.

What will they do with this wealth? Will they give any of it to the work of the church? Some will. Others will handle it as the rich young farmer did in building larger barns.

You have an opportunity to impact whether persons leave some of that $11 trillion to the work of the church, denominational institutions, the work of the International Mission Board, or the work of the North American Mission Board. Capable leaders are available to assist your church in informing members how to give to these and other causes. Contact Church Stewardship Services at 1-615-251-2497 for information.

Saving for Retirement

The U.S. savings rate fell to 3.8% in 1997, the lowest point in 58 years.[4] "The median (typical) household in America has a net worth of less than $15,000, excluding home equity. Factor out equity in motor vehicles, furniture, and such, and guess what?"[5] There is not a security net to fall back on in case of emergencies.

Social Security provides some help, but it will not make up the difference with the average American life span now at 75.5 years.[6] If inflation increases at a 3% yearly rate, a $1,100 per month Social Security payment would have to increase to $1,484 in the 10 years from age 65 to 75 to equal $1,100 in 1998.

Other factors must also be considered. Medical needs increase with aging. Medicare does not cover prescription medication. Supplemental insurance policies do cover some medication, but the monthly insurance costs increase at a much higher percentage. Nursing home care is another potential drain on savings. Few seniors have nursing home insurance.

What do these facts mean to your ministry? Several implications emerge.

- inadequate income for your senior adults
- decreased financial support for the church
- increased responsibility for the church to provide help
- increased responsibility for adult children to provide support
- dependent lifestyles and a diminished quality of life for seniors
- seniors selling their homes in order to generate cash

Potential Sources of Retirement Funds

Churches can help seniors plan ahead by acquainting them with potential sources of income when they retire. As we consider each source, we will give the financial implications for the church as well as the individual.

Social Security–Statistics show that for most retirees, the primary source of income is Social Security. This income usually increases at some percentage relative to inflation. The average Social Security monthly income for the retired worker increased from $702 in 1995 to $720 in 1996. When both husband and wife receive Social Security benefits, the combined average is $1,215. Social Security income seniors receive is directly related to their salary income before eligibility.

Expected Social Security Benefits	
Annual Earnings	Approx. Monthly Benefit (Value in Today's Dollars)
$10,000	$500
$20,000	$750
$30,000	$910
$40,000	$1,030
$50,000	$1,130
$60,000+	$1,200[7]

Get a pencil and paper or calculator. Take a tithe or 10 percent of the middle and highest Social Security income figure from the chart. A tithe of $910 is $91. Follow the figures below to determine how the church's average monthly income can be affected by those persons receiving only Social Security in retirement. Follow the progression of the considerations in the diagram below.

A Sample Church	
Total Church Budget	$200,000
Total Active Membership	150
Percentage of Membership 55+	33% or 50 members

When these persons retire to live on Social Security benefits only, consider the effect on church budget receipts. If six persons retire at age 65 and tithe on their Social Security only (as compared to receiving twice that amount before retirement), how much will the church budget decrease? This change will result in a decrease of tithe to the church of over $600 per month. For some churches this amount is close to the cost of the utility bills. How would your church be affected?

The solution to this potential church budget reduction can be corrected through the following actions: (1) careful planning based on informed projections; (2) specific education of church members using courses available through Church Stewardship Services at LifeWay Christian Resources; (3) involving more of your church members in the church budgeting process; (3) training your stewardship committee to function with vision and foresight. Refer to page 198 for specific committee training suggestions.

The solution for the person or couple living on a fixed Social Security amount is to discover additional sources of income. The two ideas given below should be considered in pre-retirement planning. Obviously, an individual cannot wait until retirement to think about company retirement plans or building a savings account.

Employer Retirement Plans—Many employers offer retirement coverages, such as the one offered to church employees through the Annuity Board of the Southern Baptist Convention. Sometimes these benefits have an inflationary factor built in, while others are fixed. Those without an inflationary factor will reduce in value in direct proportion to inflation.

If there is an inflationary factor of 3.5%, a $1,000 per month income will increase to $1,418.34 in 10 years. If there is no inflation factor, that $1,000 will reduce in value to $582 in 10 years. A good pension at the time of retirement can become worth very little by the time a person retiring at 62 reaches 77. That same $1,000 is worth $311 in 15 years with no inflation factor.

This decreasing income will also directly affect the income of your church. Since persons 55 and older give 80% of the money your church receives, you have only a few options in order to continue receiving the income needed for budget allocations.

1. Reach more people. Of course, we should reach people with the gospel because of the evangelistic assignment given by Jesus in the Great Commission.

2. Teach younger adults, teenagers, and children to be good stewards. Contact Church Stewardship Services of LifeWay Christian Resources for courses you can offer.

3. Provide educational opportunities for those approaching senior adulthood to help them invest their income to win over inflation. As they succeed, your church budget will also increase.

Income on Savings—Savings plans provide various levels of income. While Certificates of Deposit (CDs) pay the lowest returns, they are considered safest. *Safe* is a relative term. Safety with security of equity is only one kind of safety.

During the late 1970s and early 1980s, CD interest rates were as high as 18%—a good return. But as rates dropped, the income dropped until most retirees had to begin taking money from the principal.

The following illustration helps me understand the concept of return on investment. In the past, many rural families produced their own chickens. They had to decide to either eat eggs for a long time or have one meal by killing the chicken. Compare the interest on the principal to the eggs. Compare the chicken to the principal. For long-term retirement needs, the chicken needs to be able to lay eggs for the entire time in a dependable manner, or you need more chickens.

Income from Unusual Sources

Reverse mortgages can be a source of income–An additional source of income can be in the form of monthly payments based on the equity in a person's home. An individual or couple does not have to sell the home but can begin using their assets accumulated in the home. At the time of this writing, all states but Texas allow an equity line of credit. Texas homeowners can receive other loans. Choose a lender with the seal of approval of the nonprofit National Center for Home Equity Conversion (NCHEC). Reverse mortgages apply a credit line against the home equity, which gives the homeowner access to extra cash. Repayment normally is not required as long as the homeowner lives in the house.[9] When the couple or individual leaves the house permanently, it is usually sold and the proceeds used to repay the loan. If there are funds remaining, these funds become part of the homeowner's estate.

The following example shows how this plan works.
- $100,000 Home
- 70% reverse equity loan giving them the right to borrow up to $70,000
- Age of the person–70
- Approximate remaining lifetime–15 years
- 15 years x 12 monthly income payments =
    <u>180 income payments</u>

$70,000 divided by 180 equals $388 per month.

This additional source of income can make a major difference in the cash flow of persons on a limited income and still not endanger their assets. For a list of approved lenders, send $1 and a self-addressed, business-size stamped envelope to: NCHEC Preferred, Room 115, 7373 147th St., Apply Valley, MN 55124.

Loans against paid-up life insurance–This loan works when someone buys the right to collect the insurance in whole or in part at the time of death. Usually, the amount sold is only a portion and not the entire value of the policy. Before your seniors take this step, they should first withdraw the cash value from life insurance policies that have cash values. Term policies do not have cash value.

These funds can be an immediate source of cash. Seniors need a lawyer to represent them when this type transaction is chosen. These loans can be justified when warranted by financial needs. Otherwise, the policy will pay to an heir.

Persons do not normally consider reverse mortgages or life insurance loans as sources of income. You can offer an estate planning seminar where the seniors and the church can gain a complete understanding of available options.

Some persons are buying life insurance policies where their church is the named beneficiary. In this way, they leave a heritage with lasting value. One approach is to use the insurance to set up a trust for persons entering college or seminary.

The costs of the insurance policy can be deducted from the contributor's taxable income for income tax purposes. Consult with your tax advisors on how to handle this and related questions.

Another Career or Part-Time Job

Seniors have contributions to make that extend beyond their primary professions. More and more employers are turning to seniors because of their work ethic and dependability. Many employers like to hire the senior who has need for supplemental income. The employer doesn't provide benefits; however, persons working for earned income have the potential to increase their monthly Social Security income benefits.

How Much Is Enough

How much does a person need to add per month to his or her income to provide more independence and financial security? If a person retires at age 62, plan as if he will live to be 85 years old. He will need enough money with the interest and principal being used to provide a monthly income for 23 years. To calculate, use a conservative interest rate of 8%. Build in an inflation factor of 3.5% per year. In month one of year one the senior needs $189,804 using principal and interest to last until age 85, when it will be completely depleted.

Added to a $1,100 Social Security benefit, the principal and interest on the savings provides a monthly income in 1998 dollars of $2,200. A spouse would add approximately $600.00 to the income from Social Security.

The problem is that most seniors do not have even close to $189,804 to provide the additional monthly income over Social Security benefits. The average savings for retirement through pension plans and personal savings is $61,672,[8] falling far short of the need. This amount will be depleted within the first five years of retirement and does not allow for major purchases or emergencies.

Other savings are often in the form of mutual funds or similar long-term investments which have averaged approximately 12% returns over the last 10 years. This type of savings has a greater return, but for some persons the risk tolerance also increases.

Each senior and pre-senior needs to make plans based on personal goals, family needs, known medical needs, and income plans. Your church is in a position to offer financial planning as a ministry. Churches receive many contacts from companies wishing to conduct seminars to reach the church market and increase their customer base. Your role as a leader includes protecting your members from those who are more concerned for their sales than for the long-term financial needs of seniors. Contact Church Stewardship Services to obtain the names of persons in your area capable of helping you and your senior adults plan wisely.

Encourage Financial Preparations for Death

In addition to planning for retirement income, seniors in your church need to determine how they want their estates handled when they die. The modern taboo concerning talking about one's death presents a major obstacle to responsible biblical stewardship. Church leaders can set the tone for recognizing and accepting the inevitability of death. Share your own preparation for death as you have opportunity.

Although churches provide ministry during and after a death to help persons handle grief, seldom is anything done to provide help for making immediate financial decisions. Often when a spouse dies, the remaining spouse did not have primary responsibility for managing financial matters. Unfortunately, in many cases that person did not participate in family financial decisions and, therefore, does not know how to handle them.

This predicament is reason enough to encourage financial preparations for death. Here are some suggestions.

• Offer churchwide estate planning conferences with opportunities for personal appointments with an expert.

• Enlist key members to give testimonies at worship services, emphasizing the need for a proper will and estate plan.

• Conduct a "Plan Your Will" emphasis led by a competent professional. January is a popular time of the year to emphasize wills but be open to that need at any time of the year.

Here are a few legal terms and explanations you need to know in order to adequately complete estate planning:

Intestate—This term means to die without a will. In such cases the government determines how the estate is distributed. Judges try to be fair, but personal wishes and desires of the deceased are impossible to follow. As a result, the property is often disposed of at auction. Then the money is divided among the heirs.

Executor—If a person dies intestate, the courts appoint an executor. This person usually derives income for handling disposition of an estate; therefore, part of the estate is used up in fees.

Will—A will determines disposition of a person's property, including who becomes responsible for minor children. When you move from state to state, you need to have your will written for the new state.

A will can be written to include a person's church or mission interests, but this information needs to be clearly spelled out. If no will exists and the government handles the assets, religious causes will probably not be possible benefactors. Good intentions cannot provide for a church—only a will can.

Wills can state that the individual wants an asset of her estate, such as a certain mutual fund account, to be given to the church or that she wants her house used for a furloughing missionary.

A person may write out his will, prepare it with a specialized computer program, or use someone's existing will as an example. It is generally best to use an attorney, who can properly include all matters. For example, there can be complex implications if a husband and wife die in the same accident and it is hard to determine which one died first. A well-written will can help family members avoid that type of problem.

A will can be written in such detail as to define who receives individual items such as the china, bedroom furniture, money in the bank, the home, a coin collection in a drawer, or any other asset.

Tax Liability—Large estates can incur large tax liabilities. Wills and estate planning documents should be written and designed to consider taxes, as well as assets disposition and guardianship. The individual needs, wishes, and plans must be personalized to protect the assets as much as possible. In some cases, a more detailed estate plan must be written with expert legal advice. Some states also charge an inheritance or estate tax. These taxes can be legally prevented through proper estate planning. In fact, larger amounts can be protected from gift or inheritance taxes. But if proper planning is not done, these taxes will be incurred.

Personal life insurance is part of an estate. This is a little known fact, yet, if properly handled, life insurance can prevent high inheritance taxes at death. With increasing real estate values, life insurance, and other valuables, a person's estate could easily increase to the point where it will be taxed.

Living Will—A living will relates to health issues not financial issues. Persons often desire to make specific decisions regarding whether or not to use life-support equipment in the event of their illness or an accident. A living will needs to be on file with the family doctor, the local hospital, and with area or state government offices. It can also be recorded at the county courthouse.

If health care decisions are not determined by the loved one previous to his or her illness or accident, then family members must decide. They are already dealing with grief, which complicates the decisions. Even with good counseling from the doctors and pastors, these decisions are difficult.

There are legal implications as well. Often, family members have to sign agreements not to hold the hospital, doctors, and medical staff responsible.

Medical Power of Attorney—After a living will is drawn, take an additional legal step. Ask an attorney to write a Medical Power of Attorney which gives a family member the legal right to make medical decisions as if he were the person with the illness or injury. This power of attorney does not extend beyond medical issues. My brother living near my mother has Medical Power of Attorney. I have a durable power of attorney to cover business responsibilities.

Your role as a leader of seniors is to provide education so they can consider each of these issues before the problems arise. Too many persons wait until the middle of the crisis to face these critical matters.

Special Giving Methods for Persons Investing for Eternity

The stewardship responsibilities of a church include building creditability and integrity in how its resources are managed. Church leaders like yourself have the potential to fully fund additional ministries and continue present ministries by helping seniors include your church in their estate plans. There are several ways persons can leave an inheritance to their church without sacrificing their personal needs. The three listed below are not an exhaustive list, but they demonstrate that there are creative ways that will work.

A life insurance policy is a good way persons with or without money can give to the work of their church. A person can assign an existing insurance policy to the church and make regular offerings to pay for that policy. A person can also give a paid-up life insurance policy. These contributions are tax deductible, if handled correctly from the person's taxable income. A person can obtain a new insurance policy with the church as the owner while he or she gives the money to the church to pay for the policy, but be sure this policy is designed to meet IRS rules. You need to check with your church's accountant to be sure this is handled properly.

Charitable Remainder Trusts allow the owners to retain a lifetime income from the estate with the amount remaining after death going to the church. Trusts may be tax deductible when properly handled. Another type allows the income to be given to the church with the remainder going to another heir at the owner's death.

Charitable Gift Annuity Plan allows a steward to give a large gift to his or her church with the right to receive interest for two persons for a lifetime.

Encourage your seniors to think in terms of leaving a legacy. Here are some pointers when encouraging each of these types of gifts:

- Earn the right to be trusted with large gifts by knowing how to properly use them in ministry.
- Design ways for persons to give to church ministries other than the budget. A church that designs all giving around the budget will miss many large gifts. Persons with large gifts will give to their church if they see how the church will use their generosity for the greatest potential. Like it or not, most people do not tithe. This does not mean that they do not have a generous streak and tender heart when it comes to the Lord's work.
- Design ways for persons to be challenged beyond budget giving. The Lord may be impressing upon you or me to give a particular gift, but will we hear, if our gifts do not fit the "box" of the budget? We must learn to paint outside the budget lines.
- Offer opportunities for persons to give targeted gifts. Recently I received a request for persons who would be capable of paying their own way for an overseas mission trip to equip persons in the use of *MasterLife*. The request was for Finland, a newer area of mission work. Within two days, two persons were ready to go. One paid his own way, and the other had his way paid by a fellow church member.
- Learn to see the activity of God in the challenges around you. God always asks us to do what we cannot do in our own strength. When God issues a challenge, don't look for visibly available funds. Look at the opportunity to see how God provides, for He surely will. One reason most churches do not see the supernatural activity of God is that they do not include the supernatural in their plans.

Consider Volunteerism As Stewardship

Most traditional volunteerism involves enlisting church members to help with tasks around the church, from cleaning to construction of a building. Be flexible to allow creative and functional approaches to volunteerism as a means of stewardship. The possibilities are unlimited. Help your seniors dream God-sized dreams, therefore seizing God-sized opportunities.

Recently I talked to a friend who is in the process of donating a large gift to his church. He and several other members of his church in building trades are volunteering their expertise and labor to help him build a $200,000 house. When the house is sold, the profits will be given to the church. He expects to recover only his material costs. The house is deeded to the church from the beginning of construction. As the general contractor, he will oversee the construction and his company will warranty the home so the church will not have that responsibility. The net profit to the church will be approximately $100,000. This is a non-traditional method of volunteerism which is exciting to consider.

Retired computer technicians can establish a business and give the proceeds from one day or one week of each month to the church. Several churches can pool their volunteers to establish many kinds of businesses.

Groups may pool their various skills with the intent to start a church on a foreign mission field each year or more often from the proceeds of a volunteer-based business. What a sense of fulfillment it would be for the building team to go to the site for a week of visitation, training, and revival!

A word of caution is appropriate when it comes to volunteerism. Persons may volunteer to do work for which they are not skilled. Volunteerism must be managed by a skilled leader.

Many cities have a building codes department that monitors construction of buildings. Church buildings are considered commercial construction and must meet the codes. A violation citation is not good stewardship nor a good witness to the community. In order for the problem to be corrected, the church will spend double the money it would have spent in doing the job properly the first time.

An attempt to save money can become bad stewardship. Not all volunteerism is good stewardship.

Your Stewardship Committee may be willing to determine what it would have cost for volunteer work to be done by local businesses and report the amount to the church as an addendum to the financial gifts. Be sure to emphasize that volunteer labor is in addition to, and not a substitute for, regular tithes and gifts.

Plan Your Church's Response

While society as a whole places a decreasing value on seniors, this attitude should not be true of God's bride, the church. Seniors will quickly discern manipulation if your motives to help them with stewardship issues are not pure. Your genuine concern for them can be expressed by assisting them in making good financial plans.

You may not be in their generation and may not understand their caution and hesitancy to make these types of decisions. They make decisions based on values. For example, we may consider their closets and garages to be filled with "junk." They save these items because they might need them someday. Remember that some seniors as of this writing survived the Great Depression. As you provide a financial planning ministry, take into consideration their values as well as more utilitarian concerns.

Tithing is still a valid biblical message for today and any day.

> Trust in the Lord with all your heart and lean not on your own understanding; in all your ways acknowledge him, and he will make your paths straight. Do not be wise in your own eyes; fear the Lord and shun evil. This will bring health to your body and nourishment to your bones. Honor the Lord with your wealth, with the firstfruits of all your crops; then your barns will be filled to overflowing, and your vats will brim over with new wine (Prov. 3:5-10).

Encourage your pastor when the Lord leads him to preach on stewardship. Follow-up these messages with periodic financial planning seminars/workshops for seniors and the church family as a whole. The following topics should be offered on a rotating basis.

- Estate planning
- Transfer of wealth
- Retirement income
- Preparing taxes
- Social Security
- Financial planning
- Budget planning
- Making a will
- Investments
- Pre-retirement planning

Give the Stewardship Committee a Larger Vision

A stewardship committee with responsibilities that extend beyond the church budget will help you retain the present senior, enlist the emerging senior, prepare the next generation senior, and be ready for future seniors. Your church will benefit from expanding the organizational design, purpose, and views of this committee.

The term *stewardship committee* is not another name for the finance committee. The term *stewardship committee* gets its focus and work from the Great Commission. Stewardship involves one's entire life: money, relationships, values, work and service.

A visionary stewardship committee can transform the mindset of your church to a focus on possibilities, not limitations. Most church stewardship committees review their previous year's budget to determine by what percentage they can increase the next year's budget. Good stewardship training challenges church members beyond where their faith has previously taken them.

The ministries of a church should not be driven by the financial cost of doing the work. It should be based in a spirit of generosity that generates from a personal relationship with Christ. It is the work of the Kingdom of God where Christ Jesus is the King and church members are His servants.

Therefore, a church stewardship committee should focus on what can be called ministry action budgeting. Some of these ministries can be done by volunteers, while other ministries require funding. When you fund the activity of God, you are surely joining the Lord Jesus in His work. Let visionary members lead the way as you help the committee function from a spiritual perspective.

The Church Stewardship Committee has specific responsibilities.

- stewardship education that disciples believers to be God's asset managers
- budget development and promotion focusing on the activity of God
- budget and financial management done with competence and integrity
- estate stewardship with an expanding world mission view

Depending upon the size of your church, you can have four subcommittees with assignments in each of these responsibility areas. They might be called Stewardship Education, Budget Development and Promotion, Financial Management, and Estate Stewardship. A smaller church may choose to do only two of these assignments. For more information contact Church Stewardship Services, 127 Ninth Avenue, North, Nashville, TN 37234-0182.

---

[1] Shannon C. Dufresne, "Retirement Planning for Baby Boomers," 2 October 1995 <http://www.luca.com> (10 February 1998).

[2] "Retirement Cash Falling Short Among Baby Boomers," 9 December 1997 <http://www.womenconnect.com/personal finance> (10 February 1998).

[3] Nancy Ammerman, Emory University; *Florida Baptist Convention Stewardship Survey;* Chase Report of Atlanta, Georgia, n.d., 15-16.

[4] New York Times News Services, "American Borrowing May Be Slowing Down," *The Tennessean,* 17 February 1998, Business section, p. 2, col. 3.

[5] Thomas J. Stanley and William D. Danko, *The Millionaire Next Door* (Marietta, GA: Longstreet Press, Inc., 1996), 2.

[6] Vicky Uhland, "Retire? Boomers May Opt to Further Careers," <http://www.womenconnect.com/personal finance> (10 February 1998).

[7] Eric Tyson, *Personal Finance For Dummies, 2nd edition* (Milwaukee, WI: Christian Stewardship Association, 1996), 142.

[8] "Retirement Cash Falling Short Among Baby Boomers," 9 December 1997 <http://www.womenconnect.com/personal finance> (10 February 1998).

[9] Jane Bryant Quinn, "The Right Lender for a Reverse Mortgage," 5 January 1998 <http://www.washingtonpost.com> (10 February 1998).

Chapter 11

A Strategic Plan for Ministry

by Joseph Northcut

What Is Strategy Planning?
Strategy Planning for Senior Adult Ministry
Characterize Senior Adults in Your Church
Characterize Senior Adults in Your Community
Develop a Ministry Plan
Rely on Kingdom Growth Principles
Implement and Evaluate the Plan

The word of the Lord came to me: "Son of man, prophesy against the shepherds of Israel; prophesy and say to them: 'This is what the Sovereign Lord says: Woe to the shepherds of Israel who only take care of themselves! Should not shepherds take care of the flock?'" (Ezek. 34:1-2).

This question "Should not shepherds take care of the flock?" has always intrigued me. Should not we as church leaders take care of the people God has placed within our circle of influence? When we begin to realize that God has entrusted to us the lives of individuals in our community, this question calls us to accountability.

What does caring involve? If we get to know people in our community and discover their needs, do we then have a responsibility to meet those needs and build relationships for sharing Christ? How does a church, once it discovers and determines the needs within the community, meet those needs?

A growing proportion of the flock in most churches consists of senior adults. Based on census statistics and demographics, communities across our nation are shifting to a large senior adult segment. Senior adults will compose the majority of many churches and the entirety of others. A church that learns how to involve and minister to this age group will be a church that will impact its community.

What Is Strategy Planning?

A strategic plan is a God-ordained process determined through prayer and study that enables us to "care for the flock." Strategy planning has been defined as imagining a future state and resourcing to achieve it. A simple definition of strategy planning is:

- identify purpose, objectives, and desired results
- establish a realistic program to obtain these results
- evaluate performance in achieving these results.

Strategy planning for senior adult ministry involves programming events and activities for maximum support with the greatest chance of success. It also establishes criteria for planning future ministries.

What Will Strategy Planning Do?

Strategy planning will:

- provide you with a written plan
- get more people involved and committed to the plan
- free up the pastor and staff to do what they are uniquely called to do
- create a productive and efficient organization.

Is Strategy Planning Biblical?

God is both creative and orderly. He established His plan of redemption from the beginning of time, works out everything in conformity to His plan, and knows how and when time will end for the fulfillment of His glory (see Eph. 1:4-14). The following Scriptures indicate that God planned His work!

> The Lord Almighty has sworn, "Surely, as I have planned, so it will be, and as I have purposed, so it will stand" (Isa. 14:24).

> What I have said, that will I bring about; what I have planned, that will I do (Isa. 46:11).

A senior adult ministry without a strategic plan will not move with steadiness and certainty toward its goals. An endless supply of distractions can rob the ministry of focus. Pursuing God's purpose and vision demands careful planning.

These Scriptures indicate God's pleasure when we plan according to His revealed will:

> May he give you the desire of your heart and make all your plans succeed (Ps. 20:4).

> Commit to the Lord whatever you do, and your plans will succeed (Prov. 16:3).

> By wisdom a house is built, and through understanding it is established (Prov. 24:3).

What Can I Expect with a Strategic Plan?

- a written plan to which everyone can refer for clarity
- commitment by the entire ministry to its overall direction
- clear job duties and responsibilities
- time for leaders to do what they have been called to do
- a strategy planning team in place to guide the ministry into its next era of growth.

What Does Strategy Planning for Ministry Involve?

The strategy planning process works for any organization which seeks to be intentional about its purpose, functions, and outcomes. Several steps are necessary to produce a strategy planning document. When a church decides to engage in strategy planning, the strategy planning team will gather data to:

1. Develop the church's mission statement.
2. Determine the characteristics of the church and community.
3. Realistically assess the church's strengths and weaknesses.
4. Identify priority issues and concerns.
5. Establish objectives that address the priority issues.
6. Make short- and long-range plans to meet objectives.
7. Evaluate plans to determine whether objectives are being met and are consistent with the priority issues and concerns.
8. Reevaluate assumptions (revisit the strategic plan) before setting objectives for the next budget year.

Strategy Planning for Senior Adult Ministry

Most churches that use a strategy planning process will include the senior adult ministry as a part of the overall plan for the church. Seek to secure the cooperation of the pastor, staff, and church leadership to participate in a churchwide process. If this is not possible, the senior adult ministry (SAM) will still benefit from completing the eight steps of a strategy planning process.

The following scenario describes the process a SAM would pursue if strategy planning is not a churchwide effort. This approach is one of several that offers beneficial results. Adapt this process to fit the needs of your SAM.

Determine the Team

The pastor, church staff member, or senior adult coordinator is the primary leader in developing the strategies for SAM, but he cannot do the work alone. He must utilize the senior adult steering committee or a specially-chosen planning team to assist in this vital task. The team then works through the strategy planning process.

Subgroups of the team may be designated to facilitate the compilation of data. Subgroups may divide the work among task assignments such as church senior adult profile; community senior adult profile; community services to seniors; pin map study; and personal interviews.

Develop a Mission Statement

Many churches have a mission statement. If your church is one of those that do, use it as the basis of the statement you will write for your SAM. SAM must "fit" beneath the umbrella of the church. SAM must not "go off on its own" but rather seek to reflect the overall direction of the total church body.

If your church does not have a mission statement in place, engage church leadership in developing one. A mission statement restates the Great Commission in contemporary terms the church can understand. It states how a particular church intends to fulfill the Great Commission in its context. It serves as motivation to minister, an anchor in times of change, and a statement of intention for believers in the church.

A mission statement combines purpose and vision. The statement needs to be concise and well-written in order to communicate with the body of believers, who eventually will follow it as their guide. The mission statement will most likely be used in church publications and planning documents.[1] Here are sample church mission statements:

- Calvary Baptist Church is a family fellowship that exists to help people find and experience God.
- West Side Baptist Church exists to exalt the Lord, evangelize the lost, and equip the laity.
- Our mission is to honor God, love people, and meet needs in the Spring Valley church and community.

Lead your SAM planning group to personalize the church's mission statement to reflect your ministry. Here is a sample SAM mission statement:

> The Mission of First Baptist Church of Norfolk Senior Adult Ministry is to honor God by providing opportunities for spiritual growth, creating opportunities for fellowship and adventure, and reaching lost and unchurched senior adults.

Characterize Senior Adults in Your Church

The second step your strategy planning team will take involves collecting data to characterize the senior adults in your church. Jesus said we are to be witnesses beginning in Jerusalem. Why would God send other senior adults to your church to care for, nurture, disciple, evangelize, and empower for service/ministry if you are not taking care of those He has already sent you?

> Be shepherds of God's flock that is under your care, serving as overseers—not because you must, but because you are willing, as God wants you to be; not greedy for money, but eager to serve; not lording it over those entrusted to you, but being examples to the flock (1 Pet. 5:2).

Assess your shepherding. Begin by identifying and analyzing the senior adults within your congregation. Effective ministry and programming begin with intensive homework. How do you identify and analyze senior adults in your church?

1. Complete a senior adult profile to determine the number of seniors, their age groupings, gender, and marital status.

   Gather the information you need from church membership records. If your records are computerized, ask the office staff to compile the information you need. Or, you may complete the profile by hand, using the following chart.

Age Group	Married	Divorced	Remarried	Widowed	Never Married	Women	Men
50-64							
65-74							
75-84							
85-up							

2. Study Sunday School records. Find seniors who are members of Sunday School but not members of the church. These seniors must be included in your SAM plan. Include their information on your senior adult profile.

3. Survey senior adults to collect specific information. Give members time before or during the Sunday School department assembly or at the beginning or end of class time to complete the survey (anonymously) and return it at that time. Mail surveys to seniors on the church roll but not active in Sunday School. Include a postage paid self-addressed envelope. A sample survey form begins on page 215. You have permission to duplicate it for use in your church.

4. Compile the statistical data you have collected in a report form. The report should clearly identify seniors in your church by number, gender, marital status, age grouping, and other pertinent demographic information taken from the survey.

5. Consider identifying neighborhoods where your seniors live by using a pin map, with each pin representing a senior member of your church or Sunday School. Noting the geographical locations of members gives you important information for follow-up of ministry needs and prospects in your community. Also use different colored pins to denote different types of housing (residence, retirement facility, nursing home, and so forth).

6. Conduct personal interviews with representative senior adults and senior adult leaders. Ask persons to identify:

- reasons senior adults attend your church
- reasons senior adults might not visit (join) your church
- perceptions of church members about senior adults
- perceptions of senior adults about the church.

7. Compile a document with an analysis of the data you have collected in order to profile the senior adult members of your church.

Characterize Senior Adults in Your Community

Once you have identified seniors in your church, look at the "fields white unto harvest" that surround the church. An acronym of the word *care* is "Caring and Reaching Everyone" or "Christ's Arms Reaching Everyone." How does a church become outward-focused so that God can use it to make a difference in the community, particularly to unreached and unsaved senior adults?

Here are some ways to identify seniors in the community:

1. Survey adult church members to gather information on their parents, other senior adult relatives, senior adult neighbors, and friends who would be prospects for your church.

2. Survey children and youth Sunday School leadership to gather information on grandparents and other senior caregivers of children and youth in your church.

3. Compile prospect lists from "Who do you know?" cards (prospect cards) available in Sunday School departments/classes or in church bulletins or pew racks.

4. Collect demographic information about senior adults in your community and immediate area. In your city library look for the current census bureau report, city planning documents, and public school planning documents. These sources identify seniors by numbers and locations in your city.

Church Community Diagnosis Workbook (ISBN 0-7673-2048-4) is available by calling the Customer Service Center at 1-800-458-2772. Strategic and growth planning assistance is available through several Southern Baptist agencies which have consultants participating in the Southern Baptist Data Consortium.

Scan/US is a software package that provides demographic information from the census report. Most Baptist state conventions have access to this software, as well as the North American Mission Board. Many state conventions also have access to PRIZM information which segments a given population into various lifestyle segments. Both Scan/US and PRIZM can be used to provide greater understanding of a community.

5. Contact community agencies and organizations that serve senior adults. Glean information from the Area Office on Aging. Talk to persons in the city planning office, Chamber of Commerce, Social Security office, and senior centers. Often, the community United Way has an information and referral directory or can give you information on senior housing and services for senior adults. Compile this information into a report.

6. Survey the community around your church door-to-door, by telephone, or both. Collect basic information such as names, addresses, phone numbers, approximate ages, marital status, and some indication of the spiritual needs of each household. The goal is to gather information which can be used by the church to achieve outreach, evangelism, and ministry objectives to senior adults as well as others discovered through this process.

   To conduct this survey, form three ministry teams:
   • Canvassing Team
   • Assignment/Packets Team
   • Records Processing Team

   Enlist a coordinator to direct the survey. The coordinator enlists a chairperson for each ministry team. Positive results will come if team members have high expectations and concern for individuals with specific spiritual needs.

   To prepare the Assignment/Packets, ask this team to gather maps and cross-reference city directories to determine the extent of the project. This group determines which areas are to be surveyed door-to-door and which by telephone (exchanges). Assignment packets should be prepared by zones and/or teams.

Materials needed for the project are survey cards, canvasser commitment cards, pencils, envelopes, maps/directories, instructions, training helps, processor's instructions, visitation assignment, and report materials. These may be purchased or produced. This project is not complete until the gathered information is available for church visitors in a prospect assignment and report form.

Prepare assignment packets prior to training meetings. Consider the abilities of each canvasser. Some may be able to canvass a larger area than others.Persons producing and assembling the packets should work closely with the persons enlisting canvassers. The coordinator should decide what material to leave at each household–a church bulletin, church promotional brochure, Sunday School lesson materials, leisure reading pieces, or perhaps a gift copy of the New Testament.

After assignment packets have been prepared, schedule training sessions for canvassers and telephoners. Make assignments according to preferences. In the training session, use role play situations that might take place during a home visit or in a telephone conversation.

Provide training for persons who will process survey data when it is submitted by canvassers. They should be familiar with all printed forms. They will check survey data and phone worksheets to sort, code, count, or tally results. This group will prepare visitation assignment forms.

Have in place a plan for immediate follow-up of prospects. Follow-up includes phone calls, visits, or a direct-mail contact with every prospect found in the survey. When the first follow-up visit is made, the person making that contact should refer to the recent area-wide survey. The outreach-evangelism director of the church should be responsible for keeping prospect information updated.

7. Complete a windshield survey of your community, where team members drive around neighborhoods near your church looking for senior adult housing, seniors in their yards, business and organizations that cater to senior adults, and so forth. Write a narrative account of your findings.

8. Based on the data you have collected, compile a report of characteristics of senior adults in your community and types of services available to them. Refer to this report as you forecast future ministry needs.

Develop a Ministry Plan

Once you have determined your target ministry population and know the services already provided to seniors in your community, you are ready to establish objectives that address priority needs. These objectives then become the basis for short- and long-range plans to meet identified needs.

Three additional actions are needed in order to determine objectives.

1. Survey senior adults during Sunday School to determine ministry needs/volunteer opportunities. Conduct the survey for two to three Sundays to ensure maximum participation. Survey, by mail or personal visits, seniors not active in Sunday School or teaching in other ages. A sample survey is found on pages 217-219.

Tabulate the results of the survey to determine types of ministries needed by senior adults. Begin a card file or computer list of persons willing to volunteer and the types of volunteer opportunities each prefers.

The senior demographic survey found on pages 215-216 can be combined with the ministry survey found on pages 217-219. If possible, give these surveys at different times several weeks apart. Seniors may find it taxing to complete both in one setting.

2. Conduct a space walk in your church building to discover space available for senior adult use. For example, is a room available for arts and craft classes during the week. Is Sunday School space adequate for projected growth? Is a nearby house or a store front a possible senior center? Write a report of your findings.

3. Conduct personal interviews with seniors representing various age groupings and degree of involvement. Interviewers are team members or their designates. Set up appointment times to correspond to times seniors would normally be at the church. Here are some sample questions that may be asked:

   What are the five strongest areas of SAM?

   What are the five weakest areas of SAM?

   What two specific programs, activities, or events would
       you like to see as a part of SAM?

   What other comments would you like to make that
       would help our planning process?

Once you identify needs and preferences of senior adults, develop a list of priority issues and concerns. You will not be able to meet all of the needs you uncover, nor will you be able to start every activity for which someone volunteers. Objectives are a necessary next step. Prayerfully consider what you can realistically hope to accomplish within the next planning cycle.

Objectives then become the basis of the strategic plan to meet those priority issues and concerns. Implementing this strategy will require leaders and members alike to understand their call to service and ministry.

Beginning a new ministry takes several months of lead time. Heed the exhortation and mandate of Ephesians 4:12 that says leaders should "prepare God's people for works of service, so that the body of Christ may be built up." Pray, enlist, and train others for ministry to and with senior adults.

Most seniors have time, skills, and experience to assist in ministry to others. Many are in good health and have few limitations.

Has each senior adult in your church identified his/her ministry gifts? How well is each serving? First Peter 4:10 says, "Each one should use whatever gift he has received to serve others, faithfully administering God's grace in its various forms."

In the memorable words of Henry Blackaby in *Experiencing God*, "Watch to see where God is working and join Him!" God is not going to hide from believers where He would like to use them in service and ministry. He will make it so very clear; our decision rests on choosing to be obedient. What God calls you to, He will equip you for; what God has equipped you for, He will call you to!

Establish one ministry at a time providing the best training and leadership to meet the needs.

Rely on Kingdom Growth Principles

One of the purposes of your strategic plan is to grow the SAM. In his book *Kingdom Principles for Church Growth*, Gene Mims identifies seven primary principles that are the foundation for church growth.[2] These same principles are applicable in developing a strong, strategic plan for SAM into the 21st century. If practiced in the spirit of honoring our Lord, these principles will offer you the opportunity to experience the power of God working in your church, community, and beyond.

Principle #1—The church must experience God and seek His kingdom; listen to God and then make decisions. As Head of the Church, God gives us our assignments. We follow His lead.

Principle #2—The kingdom of God is growing, and nothing can stop it. We can take heart; we are on the winning side!

Principle #3—God invites the church to join Him in His work of redemption. What a blessing to cooperate with God in the expansion of His kingdom! We must remember why the church exists.

Principle #4—The Great Commission is the driving force for the church. The Great Commission also should be the driving force for your SAM. God's strategic plan for us is very clear—go into the world; speak the good news of the gospel; introduce others to Christ; empower them to be the church; teach them to grow in relationship with God, others, and self; equip them to go and reach others; go without fear, for Christ is present with those who know Him; and continue going again and again into the world.

Principle #5—The Bible clearly identifies five functions of the church: evangelism, discipleship, ministry, fellowship, worship. When these five functions are applied to SAM, growth will result in four areas: numerical, spiritual, ministry, and missions.

Principle #6—Church growth methods follow God's process of kingdom growth. All that we do should reflect the nature and character of the Head of the church, Jesus Christ.

Principle #7—Church growth is God's supernatural work in a local church. It is the result of God's people obeying His will and His Word in the world.

These seven kingdom principles can serve as a philosophy for guiding your SAM to establish and achieve growth goals. A clearly defined growth strategy protects ministries from hindrances that prevent their growth. A growth strategy can also serve as a plan for coordinating all ministry strategies for your SAM.

Implement and Evaluate the Plan

Following the development of the strategic plan, the planning team should present a report to the church for approval and support. No strategy will be successful without the congregation's ownership and support.

Evaluate your strategic plan periodically—preferably monthly, quarterly, and annually. Make strategy planning an annual planning process. Use it as an ongoing evaluation tool for determining the church's ministry priorities for the coming year.

When the strategy planning process is complete, the resulting plan requires little maintenance to keep it effective and updated. Simple adjustments throughout the year are all that will be needed. This ongoing process is governed by achievable objectives customized to meet particular needs.

Benefits of Strategic Planning

The strategy planning process provides leaders with a clear picture of the church's strengths. As leaders capitalize on the church's strengths, SAM will advance from a position of strength. Conversely, the process uncovers weaknesses or gaps in providing for the needs of seniors. Strategy planning allows these gaps to be filled with effective, balanced, and growth-oriented programming.

The budgeting process becomes much simpler because priorities have been established and the church agrees on needed ministries, programs, and activities. The strategy planning process snapshots future leadership needs. This information guides future leader selection and helps place them in appropriate ministry positions.

The strategy planning process ensures effective prioritized budgeting for the senior adult ministry. The SAM budget supports and reflects the congregation's basic growth strategies.

Finally, people are motivated to participate in a ministry that is carefully planned, easily understood, communicated in various forms, and implemented consistently.

---

[1]Gene Mims and Michael Miller, *Kingdom Principles Growth Strategies: Leader's Guide* (Nashville: Convention Press, 1995), 12.
[2]Gene Mims, *Kingdom Principles for Church Growth* (Nashville: Convention Press, 1994).

SENIOR ADULT INFORMATION SURVEY

In order to minister to your needs more effectively, please take a moment to complete the following survey. Names are not required, just general information. Please feel free to give additional comments on the back of this survey.

1. I am: ❏ Married ❏ Widowed ❏ Divorced
   ❏ Remarried ❏ Never Married ❏ Other_____

2. I am: ❏ Male ❏ Female

3. My age is: ❏ 50-64 ❏ 65-74 ❏ 75-84 ❏ 85-up

4. My previous church background is:
   ❏ Assembly of God ❏ Methodist
   ❏ Presbyterian ❏ Catholic
   ❏ Baptist ❏ Other_____

5. I am a member of (your church name): ❏ Yes ❏ No
   I am in the process of joining. ❏ Yes ❏ No
   I am not a member, but I attend regularly. ❏ Yes ❏ No

6. I joined (your church name) in what year? _____

7. I attend (your church name) an average of __ times per month:
   ❏ 1 ❏ 2 ❏ 3 ❏ 4 ❏ 5
   ❏ 6 ❏ 7 ❏ 8 ❏ 9 ❏ 10+

8. I attend:
   ❏ Sunday Worship Service: ❏ Morning ❏ Evening
   ❏ Sunday Bible Study Class ❏ Discipleship Class
   ❏ Mid-Week Activity ❏ Other _____

215

9. I live: ❑ In the City   ❑ North of city
          ❑ South of city   ❑ East of city
          ❑ West of city

10. I live _____ miles from the church:
   ❑ less than 1   ❑ 1-4 miles   ❑ 4-7 miles
   ❑ 7-10 miles   ❑ more than 10

11. My mode of transportation:
   ❑ I own a car and drive myself.
   ❑ I depend on someone else for transportation.
   ❑ Other _____

12. My highest education level completed:
   ❑ High School   ❑ College
   ❑ Graduate School   ❑ Post-Graduate School

13. My income bracket per year is:
   ❑ $1,500-10,000   ❑ $10,000-20,000
   ❑ $20,000-30,000   ❑ $30,000-40,000
   ❑ $40,000-50,000   ❑ $50,000+

14. I presently tithe what percentage per month: _____%
   I presently do not tithe but I give _____% per month.

15. Rate the following areas of (your church name):
   Circle: 1=Needs Improvement, 2=Good, 3=Very Good

Facilities	1	2	3
Worship Services	1	2	3
Bible Study Class	1	2	3
Discipleship Class	1	2	3
Mid-Week Activity	1	2	3
Other _____	1	2	3

Survey of Interests, Abilities, and Needs

I. Check the following skills or interests you would be willing to contribute in the service of other senior adults, the church family or the community:

Homebound Ministry

___ visit homebound regularly

___ read to and/or write letters for homebound

___ deliver Sunday worship tapes/other literature

___ present Bible lesson

___ teach conference-call class

Home Repairs Ministry

___ painting

___ minor plumbing repairs

___ minor carpentry repairs

___ minor electrical repairs

___ help move heavy items

___ installations, such as smoke alarms, dead bolts, light bulbs

___ lawn care (mowing, raking, etc.)

Financial Information

___ assist with tax preparation

___ provide financial advice

___ assist with forms, such as Medicare, Social Security

___ estate planning

Nursing Home Ministry

___ visit nursing home resident on regular basis

___ lead music/Bible study

___ bake birthday cakes for residents

Other skills/interests

___ teach a craft (list specific craft_____)

___ host an international student in your home

___ teach someone to read

___ mentor someone

___ assist with physical therapy exercises

____ tutor children or youth

____ sit with an older person while his/her caregiver gets out

____ community advocacy

____ assist with housecleaning

____ deliver prepared meals to homes

____ shop for elderly

____ transportation to doctor and other appointments

____ telephone reassurance (daily call to specific persons)

____ plan/supervise recreational program

____ assist with multi-housing ministry

____ jail/prison ministry

____ disaster relief

____ clothing distribution

____ employment counseling

____ lead support groups (issue: _____)

____ other _____

II. Check the following services which you would find helpful.

____ daily contact by telephone

____ personal visits

____ transportation:

    ____ doctor appointments ____ church ____ shopping

____ household help for:

    ____ cleaning ____ lawn care ____ preparing meal

    ____ daily care ____ repairs

____ home delivered meals

____ legal assistance

____ tax assistance

____ financial advice

____ completing medical forms

____ bereavement counseling

____ support group (issue: _____)

____ other needs not listed: _____

III. Recreation/Hobbies & Crafts/Music

Fitness/Wellness
- ___ aerobics
- ___ exercise program
- ___ walking
- ___ jogging
- ___ swimming
- ___ weight training
- ___ nutrition

Hobbies/Crafts
- ___ antiques
- ___ ceramics
- ___ painting
- ___ flower arranging
- ___ sewing
- ___ leather craft
- ___ photography
- ___ basketry
- ___ quilting
- ___ genealogy
- ___ calligraphy
- ___ bird watching
- ___ puppets
- ___ drama/skits
- ___ computers

Sports/games
- ___ volleyball league
- ___ badminton
- ___ golf (miniature & regulation)
- ___ bowling league
- ___ hiking
- ___ bike trips
- ___ fishing
- ___ croquet
- ___ darts/archery
- ___ tennis
- ___ horseshoes
- ___ shuffleboard
- ___ whiffle ball games
- ___ table games (like _____)
- ___ camping
- ___ backpacking
- ___ attend sporting events
- ___ billiards

Music
- ___ choir
- ___ ensemble
- ___ handbells
- ___ instrument _____

IV. Information

Name:_____

Address:_____

Phone:_____

Age group: _____ 50-65 _____ 66--80 _____ 85-up

Does someone live with you? ____ Who? _____

Church member ____ Where? _____

Leader Guide

by Betty Hassler

Use the following suggestions to guide one 2-hour discussion or two 50-minute discussions of *Forward Together: A New Vision for Senior Adult Ministry*. In advance, provide participants a copy of the book and ask them to read it before the session(s).

The format can be adapted for large-group study by dividing participants into subgroups of no more than eight members for discussion questions. Ask one person from each small group to moderate the discussion and record responses using this leader guide. Allow time for small groups to report significant findings.

Arrange chairs in a semicircle or, for a large group, in semicircles of no more than eight chairs each. If possible, group persons so that different aspects of senior adult ministry are represented in each semicircle. Provide name tags.

Session 1 (50 mins.)

Begin with prayer. Direct participants (or each semicircle) to briefly introduce themselves, emphasizing their roles in senior adult ministry. Then share your enthusiasm for this study, pointing out the advantages of a coordinated senior adult ministry working together to accomplish its objectives.

Have participants locate chapter 1 and give page numbers as points are made and questions are discussed. If you are using subgroups, have groups begin discussing chapters 1–5.

Chapter 1

1. What implications of the "age wave" have we experienced at our church? Which do we expect to experience in the future?
2. How has our church sought to mobilize senior adults for ministry to other seniors? to the church? to the community?

3. What new vision do you sense we need to formulate in order to minister to today's seniors? baby boomer seniors?

Chapter 2

1. What is meant by a balanced senior adult ministry?
2. What lifestyle differences between senior adults do we see in our church?
3. How does our organization compare/contrast with the one given on pages 25-26?

Chapters 3–5

Ask these two questions of each chapter:

1. How are we meeting the needs of senior adults in this area? How should we adapt to meet the needs of younger seniors?
2. Which of the suggested ministries are available to our members? Is there one or more we need to begin?

Small-Group Reports (optional)

Ask group leaders to report one or two key ideas from each chapter without duplicating what others have said. Dismiss to break.

Break (20 mins.)–Refreshments are optional.

Session 2 (50 mins.)

Chapters 6–9

Ask the two questions given above for chapters 3–5.

Chapter 10

1. What did you learn about finances you feel other seniors need to know? How can we best get this information to them?

Chapter 11

1. What is our current planning process? Which elements of a strategy planning process do we already use?
2. Does our church (and/or senior adult ministry) need a comprehensive strategy planning process? What are some benefits?

Small-Group Reports (optional)

Following the reports on chapters 6-11, close with prayer.

Where Do I Go for Information?

Action, 1100 Vermont Avenue, NW, Washington, DC 20525

Administration on Aging, Wilbur J. Cohen Building,
330 Independence Avenue, SW, Washington, DC 20201

American Association of Homes and Services for the Aging
901 E. Street, NW, Suite 500, Washington, DC 20004-2837

American Association of Retired Persons (AARP)
1201 E Street, NW, Washington, DC 20049

American Health Care Association
1201 L Street, NW, Washington, DC 20005

American Society of Aging (ASA)
833 Market Street, San Francisco, CA 94103

Elderhostel, 75 Federal St., Boston, MA 02110-1941

Gerontological Society of America
1275 K Street, NW, Suite 350, Washington, DC 20005-4006

National Association of Area Agencies on Aging
1112 16th St., NW, Suite 100, Washington, DC, 20036

The National Council on the Aging (NOCA)
409 3rd Street, SW, Suite 200, Washington, DC 20024

National Interfaith Coalition on Aging
298 South Hull Street, Athens, GA 30605

CHRISTIAN GROWTH STUDY PLAN

Preparing Christians to Serve

In the **Christian Growth Study Plan (formerly Church Study Course),** this book *Forward Together: A New Vision for Senior Adult Ministry* is a resource for course credit in three **Leadership and Skill Development** diploma plans. To receive credit, read the book, summarize the chapters, show your work to your pastor, a staff member or church leader, then complete the information on the next page. Please check the courses for your credits. The form may be duplicated. Send the completed page to:

Christian Growth Study Plan
127 Ninth Avenue
Nashville, TN 37234-0117
FAX: (615)251-5067

For information about the Christian Growth Study Plan, refer to the current Christian Growth Study Plan Catalog. Your church office may have a copy. If not, request a free copy from the Christian Growth Study Plan office (615/251-2525).

☐ LS – 0034 (Senior Adult Ministry)
☐ LS – 0067 (Family Ministry)
☐ LS – 0083 (Church Leadership)

PARTICIPANT INFORMATION

Social Security Number (USA ONLY)	Personal CGSP Number*	Home Phone	Date of Birth (MONTH, DAY, YEAR)

Name (First, Middle, Last)

☐ Mr.   ☐ Miss
☐ Mrs.

Address (Street, Route, or P.O. Box) | City, State, or Province | Zip/Postal Code

CHURCH INFORMATION

Church Name

Address (Street, Route, or P.O. Box) | City, State, or Province | Zip/Postal Code

CHANGE REQUEST ONLY

☐ Former Name

☐ Former Address | City, State, or Province | Zip/Postal Code

☐ Former Church | City, State, or Province | Zip/Postal Code

Signature of Pastor, Conference Leader, or Other Church Leader | Date

*New participants are requested but not required to give SS# and date of birth. Existing participants, please give CGSP# when using SS# for the first time. Thereafter, only one ID# is required. **Mail to:** Christian Growth Study Plan, 127 Ninth Ave., North, Nashville, TN 37234-0117. Fax: (615)251-5067